STALAG 17

STALAG 17

BILLY WILDER

screenplay by
BILLY WILDER
EDWIN BLUM

with an introduction by
JEFFREY MEYERS

UNIVERSITY OF CALIFORNIA PRESS
BERKELEY / LOS ANGELES / LONDON

University of California Press
Berkeley and Los Angeles, California

University of California Press, Ltd.
London, England

Library of Congress Cataloging-in-Publication Data

Wilder, Billy, 1906–
    Stalag 17 / Billy Wilder ; with an introduction
    by Jeffrey Meyers.
      p.   cm.
    Includes bibliographical references.
    ISBN 0-520-21857-4 (pbk. : alk. paper)
    1. Stalag 17 (Motion picture).   II. Title.
PN1997.S6574 1999
    791.43′72—dc21   98-33437
                                       CIP

Manufactured in the United States of America
9 8 7 6 5 4 3 2 1

INTRODUCTION TO
STALAG 17

JEFFREY MEYERS

I

LIKE VLADIMIR NABOKOV, another brilliant exile and outsider, the cosmopolitan and urbane Billy Wilder had a highly idiosyncratic view of the radically different culture he encountered in America. His screenplays, like Nabokov's novels, have a fresh idiom and coruscating style. In a fifty-year career Wilder has shown astonishing versatility— and real genius—as both coauthor and director (beginning in 1943) of films about war, murder, alcoholism, Hollywood, sensational journalism, prison camps, trials and aviation, as well as of dazzling romantic comedies like *Some Like It Hot* and bittersweet love stories like *The Apartment*. His last film was *Buddy Buddy* (1981). He was also able to inspire great performances from previously undistinguished actors: Fred MacMurray and Barbara Stanwyck in *Double Indemnity*, Ray Milland in *The Lost Weekend*, William Holden in *Sunset Boulevard*. Three years later Holden won an Oscar for best actor in *Stalag 17* (1953). Wilder himself was nominated for twenty-one Academy Awards and won six.

Wilder was born in 1906 in Sucha (thirty miles south of Kraków) in Polish Galicia, then part of the Austro-Hungarian Empire. He grew up in a decadent, corrupt society torn by class conflicts and unstable institutions. As a child he witnessed the collapse of the empire after World War I and acquired a sardonic view of the frailty of personal relations. The son of a hotelier and small-time businessman, he briefly studied law at the University of Vienna, then became a newspaper reporter, first in Vienna and later in Berlin, where he supplemented his income by working as a dance-partner and gigolo. With Robert Siodmak and Fred Zinnemann, he made the German documentary *People on Sunday* (1929). When Hitler came to power in 1933, Wilder fled to Paris and directed his first feature film, *Mauvaise Graine (Bad Seed)*, with Danielle Darrieux. He reached Hollywood in 1934, and roomed with a fellow exile, Peter Lorre.

Wilder arrived in America with no knowledge of English apart from some obscenities and snatches of popular songs. He learned the new language in the same practical way as the Austrian-born director Fritz Lang. "I read a lot of newspapers," Lang recalled, "and I read comic strips—from which I learned a lot. I said to myself, if an audience—year in, year out—reads so many comic strips, there must be something interesting in them. And I found them very interesting. I got . . . an insight into the American character, into American humour; and I learned slang. I drove around in the country and tried to speak with everybody. I spoke with every cab driver, every gas station attendant—and I looked at films."[1]

Explaining his need for a coauthor, Wilder said: "I started the idea of collaborating when I first arrived in America, because I could not speak the language. I needed somebody who was responsible, who had some idea of how a picture is constructed. Then I found out that it's *nice* to have a collaborator—you're not writing into a vacuum, especially if he's sensitive and ambitious to create a product of some value."[2] After several years of screenwriting hackwork—*Music in the Air*, *Lottery Lover*, *Champagne Waltz*—his career took off in 1938 when he began his long and fruitful collaboration with Charles Brackett. They began with witty and intelligent movies like *Bluebeard's Eighth Wife*, *Ninotchka*, and *Ball of Fire* and ended with their greatest film, *Sunset Boulevard* (1950).

Between his long-term partnerships with Brackett and I. A. L. Diamond, Wilder wrote *Stalag 17* with Edwin Blum, an experienced screenwriter and friend with whom he often played tennis and bridge. Though their collaboration was successful and the film made $10 million the first year, Blum found the experience agonizing. Blum said that he regarded himself as "little more than [Wilder's] butler. It was his screenplay. My name is on the credits but I don't think of it as mine. Oh, I made important contributions, especially in developing Sefton. When you work with Billy he rules you a thousand percent. I couldn't take insults. I wouldn't work with him on another picture. I know he is a man that the more he likes you, the more sarcastic he gets, but I couldn't take it." Twenty-five years later, and still licking his wounds, Blum recalled Wilder's caustic remark: "I have this cretin collaborating with me. Listen to the rotten words he uses. . . . That is not good enough, Eddie. When I had Charlie Brackett as my partner, he came up with exquisite words. . . . He was literate. That is the kind of writer I was working with. A literate man. Not an ignoramus like you."[3]

Emphasizing the roles he could play while directing, Wilder said: "I can become a masochist. I can become the Marquis de Sade. I can become a midwife. I can become Otto Preminger. I can do all sorts of things. It depends on what will work on actors."[4] Wilder planned all the camera shots while writing the script, and never let the actors deviate from his text. Just as he had used an Austrian director, Erich von Stroheim, in *Sunset Boulevard*, so he cast another Austrian director, the Jewish Otto Preminger, in the role of the camp Kommandant, Colonel von Scherbach, in *Stalag 17*.

Wilder joked, "I have to be nice to Preminger because I still have relatives in Germany,"[5] but kept the upper hand in their film. "He always forgot his lines," Wilder recalled. "He was very strict when he was a director, but he himself . . . [h]e said, 'Forgive me, I'm a little rusty,' and in the evening he always sent you three pounds of caviar. Very generous."[6] In the film von Scherbach wears a luxurious fur collar on his immaculate uniform, puts on high boots so he can click his heels when talking on the phone to Berlin, and walks on specially laid planks while everyone else steps through the mud. At the end of the picture, however, he too wades through the mud and discovers that his spy has been killed.

The basis of the film, Donald Bevan and Edmund Trzcinski's play, *Stalag 17*, was directed by José Ferrer and opened on Broadway in May 1951. John Ericson played Sefton, while Robert Strauss (Animal) and Harvey Lembeck (Shapiro) appeared in both the play and the film. Wilder developed the play and made it more interesting in every way.

In the play the Kommandant issues orders but never appears; in the film Wilder makes him one of the most important characters. The first attempt to escape and the killing of Manfredi and Johnson, as well as the harsh interrogation of Dunbar, take place offstage in the play but are dramatized in the film. Taking advantage of film's ability to focus on tiny objects in a close-up, Wilder has Schulz and Price leave their notes in a hollow chess piece rather than under a loose brick. The prisoners' insult, "Drop dead," becomes the comic "Droppen Sie dead." Dunbar is an officer, rather than a sergeant-major, to intensify his conflict with Sefton. Wilder, in fact, invented the most memorable aspects of the film: Sefton's mouse race, his private schnapps distillery, and his telescope-observatory to watch the bathhouse of the female Russian prisoners. "You couldn't catch much through that steam," the narrator observes, "but believe you me, after two years in that camp just the idea what was behind that steam sure spruced up your voltage." Wilder also thought up the telltale light cord, as well as Sefton's trunk of luxury goods, his bets against prisoners who try to escape, and his great exit line.

Wilder's conclusion is also superior to the play's. In the stage version, as Hoffy says, Dunbar "came back to the barracks to pick up his gear so we slipped his guard a doped-up drink and sneaked Dunbar out of the barracks."[7] In the film, however, Dunbar is snatched from his SS guards when the prisoners explode a smoke bomb made from thousands of ping pong balls. And Price is unmasked by Sefton, who uses Price to help Dunbar escape.

The film was also influenced by Jean Renoir's *Grande Illusion* (1937). In both pictures prisoners of war dig a tunnel to escape, desperately try to amuse themselves and avoid boredom, and maintain a light-hearted attitude in order to survive. They put on a show (some dressed in women's clothes) and sing a patriotic song to keep up their spirits. They are friendly with the German guard, who is rather comic in his rigid militarism, and even manage to control him. And the intravenous line that hangs down after Boeldieu's death inspired the looped and hanging light cord in *Stalag 17*.

Wilder's film, however, is quite different from Renoir's humanistic, antiwar expression of international brotherhood. He transforms the chivalric self-sacrifice of the officer class into a bitter drama of egoism and betrayal. The prisoners become divided among themselves, and their traditional camaraderie is destroyed. Instead of uniting against their oppressors—as in classic prisoner of war pictures like *The Bridge on the River Kwai* (1957) and *The Great Escape* (1963)—the men find their personal and class conflicts accentuated rather than transcended in the camp. In the end the prisoners succeed, not because of their superior values, but because of Sefton's cold intelligence.

▮▮

The film opens as armed German guards walk along a high barbed-wire fence with fierce-looking dogs. Stalag 17 (short for *Stamm Lager*, or "prison camp") is located near the Danube in Austria and filled with sergeants in the American air force. The time is Christmas week 1944, and on the secret radio the prisoners hear accounts of the Battle of the Bulge—the last great German offensive in World War II. The men in the harsh yet almost cozy-looking barracks are bored, tense, and nervous, resigned yet never hopeless. They have dug a tunnel and devised an elaborate escape. Two airmen plan to break out and travel to Krems, forty miles northwest of Vienna, along the river to Linz and Ulm, in southern Germany, then by train to Friedrichshafen on the north shore of Lake Constance and finally—as in Hemingway's *A Farewell to Arms*—across the lake by rowboat to Switzerland. But the detailed plan fails and the men, shot while trying to escape, never get out of the camp. As von Scherbach insists: "Nobody has ever escaped from Stalag 17. Not alive, anyway."

Like *Double Indemnity* and *Sunset Boulevard*, *Stalag 17* is narrated by a voice-over. And there are other characteristic Wilder touches: Sefton keeps striking matches, like Fred MacMurray in *Double Indemnity*, and an old Plymouth (which Wilder may have once owned) is repossessed in both *Sunset Boulevard* and (as Shapiro learns through letters from home) in *Stalag 17*.

After carefully calculating the odds, Sefton attracts hostility and suspicion by betting that the prisoners won't escape. Better dressed than all the others, he wears boots, a hat, and gloves. He owns toilet articles, eats a precious fried egg for breakfast, and generously gives away the empty shells. After bribing the guards, he has sex with the Russian women and then boasts about it. He thrives in the camp while others are oppressed and defeated. His egoistic attitude—"This is everybody for himself. Dog eat dog"—is savagely Darwinian.

Sefton cynically yet realistically opposes all attempts to escape. Even if you succeeded and got all the way back to America, he says, the air force would simply "ship you to the Pacific and slap you in another plane. And you get shot down again and you wind up in a Japanese prison camp. That's if you're lucky! Well, I'm no escape artist! You can be the heroes." Even Animal, the dumbest guy in the barracks, thinks "Maybe the Krauts knew all about that tunnel all the time!" The prisoners suspect a spy in their midst, but as in a well-constructed murder mystery, the evidence points to the wrong man.

Both playwrights and screenwriters felt the need to lighten the serious theme with farcical comedy. Sig Ruman, known for his comic roles in the Marx brothers' *Night at the Opera* and Wilder's *Ninotchka*, plays Schulz, the German sergeant, in a jovial rather than menacing manner. He expresses the ambiguity of the prisoners' situation by joking with them and bustling about with Teutonic good humor. But as the liaison with the traitor, he is also responsible for betrayals and deaths. It is absurd, in both the play and the film, for the prisoners to ask Schulz to name the informer.

Animal's crudeness and slapstick comedy (when he falls in the mud) and his obsession with Betty Grable (a wartime sex symbol, now virtually forgotten) are tediously overdone. And the Christmas dance scene is far too long. Trzcinski, coauthor of the stage version, plays Triz in the film and is poignantly effective as the airman who desperately tries to believe his wife's story of finding a baby on their doorstep. He even knits a little garment for the infant. But the film loses intensity and interest whenever the focus strays from Sefton.

The arrival of the upper-class Lieutenant Dunbar deepens the themes of class conflict and personal betrayal, and sets up the final antagonism. While being transported to the prison camp Dunbar has blown up an ammunition train in Frankfurt. Sefton, who knew and resented Dunbar in Boston and in training camp, is as hostile to the new hero as he is to the old prisoners. The tunnel and clandestine radio have already been discovered. So when Dunbar is seized by von Scherbach and accused of sabotage, the prisoners beat up Sefton—the obvious culprit—for ratting on Dunbar.

Sefton, the pariah, must discover the real spy in order to save himself. He notices that Price loops the light cord whenever he leaves a message in the black chess queen and that Schulz, after retrieving the message, unties the cord and lets it hang down and swing. Hiding in the emptied barracks, Sefton overhears Price telling Schulz, in German, how Dunbar blew up the train.

In a satisfying dramatic scene, Sefton tells the astonished prisoners that Price "lived in Cleveland, but when the war broke out he came back to the Fatherland like a good little Bundist. He spoke our lingo so they put him through spy school, gave him phony dogtags." In a neat parallel, Schulz, like Price, had also returned to Germany from America when the war broke out. The crucial question, as Sefton (but none of the others) perceives, is not so much *who* the traitor is, but "what do you do with him? You tip your mitt and the Jerries pull him out of here and plant him someplace else. . . . Or you kill him off and the Krauts turn around and kill off the whole barracks."

Since Price is a German, the horrible possibility of a traitor within, of "one American squealing on other Americans," is evaded. In the tightly constructed conclusion, Sefton devises a plan by which Price, acting as a decoy for Dunbar, enables the American to escape. Price has tin cans tied to his ankle just as Manfredi had a clothes bag tied to his, and just as the Germans shoot down the Americans in the beginning, so they kill their own spy at the end.

Sefton had said "I'm no escape artist" and bet against Dunbar's escape as he had once bet against Manfredi and Johnson's. But he now likes the odds and takes Price's place with Dunbar, though the lieutenant has been exhausted by von Scherbach's interrogation and then frozen by his long wait in the icy water tank. Before leaving, however, Sefton takes a last parting shot at his dim-witted companions by contemptuously exclaiming: "If I ever run into any of you bums on a street corner, just let's pretend we never met before. Understand?" He then succeeds, for the first time, in breaking out of the camp—alive.

Analyzing the development of Sefton's character, Wilder said: "He is the black marketeer in Stalag 17. He bet them cigarettes and whatever he could for self-aggrandizement, but then when the chips are down, you slowly change your opinion about him. You need that kind of twist. Suddenly you see that the guy they have beaten up because they think, as the audience does, that he is a shit . . . slowly, slowly he emerges as a superhero."[8] Trzcinski disliked the emphasis on Sefton's nastiness so much that he refused to speak to Wilder after the film was completed. But, as in all Wilder's best work, motives are mixed and morality is ambiguous. Focusing on the depravity of the group and on Sefton's moral isolation, François Truffaut emphasized the film's originality: "Sefton escapes to get away from the companions whom he despises rather than from a regime he has come to terms with and guards he's been able to bend to his needs. . . . For the first time in films the philosophy of the solitary man is elaborated; this film is an apologia for individualism."[9]

The final irony, Wilder later recalled, took place three years after the film was released: "I got a letter from the head of distribution saying, 'We've got good news. The Germans are crazy about *Stalag 17*. They would like to release it, but we have to make one little change: The spy that is hiding among them is not a German—make him a Pole.' And I just said: 'Fuck you, gentlemen. Haven't you got any shame? You ask me, who lost his family in Auschwitz, to do a mistake like this? Unless somebody apologizes, forget about my contract. Good-bye, Paramount.' Nobody apologized, and I left Paramount. But it remained the way it was in the American picture."[10]

NOTES

1. Quoted in Peter Bogdanovich, *Fritz Lang in America* (New York: Praeger, 1969), p. 15.

2. Quoted in Kevin Lally, *Wilder Times: The Life of Billy Wilder* (New York: Holt, 1996), p. 416.

3. Quoted in Maurice Zolotow, *Billy Wilder in Hollywood* (New York: Putnam, 1977), pp. 181, 300–301.

4. Quoted in Jay Leyda, *Voices of Film Experience: 1894 to the Present* (New York: Macmillan, 1977), p. 508.

5. Quoted in Peter Bogdanovich, *Who the Devil Made It: Conversations with Legendary Film Directors* (1997; New York: Ballantine, 1998), p. 606.

6. Quoted in Lally, *Wilder Times*, p. 224.

7. Donald Bevan and Edmund Trzcinski, *Stalag 17* (New York: Dramatists Play Service, 1951), p. 56.

8. Quoted in Lally, *Wilder Times*, p. 220.

9. François Truffaut, *The Films in My Life*, trans. Leonard Mayhew (1978; New York: Simon & Schuster, 1985), p. 163.

10. Quoted in Lally, *Wilder Times*, p. 226.

STALAG 17

<u>STALAG 17</u>

Billy Wilder
Edwin Blum

<u>FINAL WHITE</u>
January 30, 1952

PARAMOUNT PICTURES CORPORATION

P. 11490

STALAG 17

FINAL WHITE
Billy Wilder
Edwin Blum
January 30, 1952

F-23—N-8

Received from Secretarial Dept.

P. 11490
Billy Wilder
Edwin Blum
January 30, 1952

Title_____STALAG 17_____

Signed_____

PARAMOUNT PICTURES CORPORATION

5

THE AMERICANS

SEFTON .... WILLIAM HOLDEN

DUKE .... NEVILLE BRAND

HOFFY .... RICHARD ERDMAN

STOSH .... ROBERT STRAUSS

HARRY .... CY HOWARD

PRICE .... PETER GRAVES

DUNBAR .... DON TAYLOR

BAGRADIAN .... JAY LAWRENCE

TRIZ .... EDMUND TRZCINSKI

COOKIE .... GIL STRATTON, JR.

JOEY .... ROBINSON STONE

BLONDIE .... ROBERT SHAWLEY

JOHNSON .... PETER BALDWIN

MANFREDI .... MICHAEL MOORE

MARKO .... WILLIAM PIERSON

THE CRUTCH ....

AND OTHER P.O.W.s

THE GERMANS

OBERST VON SCHERBACH............ OTTO PREMINGER

SCHULZ .... SIG RUMAN

FIRST GERMAN LIEUTENANT......... CARL FORCHT

SECOND GERMAN LIEUTENANT........ HAROLD MARESCH

OFFICERS, GUARDS, SOLDIERS, S.S. MEN

THE RUSSIANS

MEN PRISONERS

WOMEN PRISONERS

THE NEUTRAL

GENEVA MAN .... ERWIN KALSER

SEQUENCE A

FADE IN:

1. <u>BARBED WIRE AGAINST A WINTRY NIGHT SKY</u>

Beyond it, more barbed wire. Ice has formed on the
strands. Now and then searchlight beams crisscross
the pattern. As the CAMERA SLOWLY MOVES along the
double fence, SUPERIMPOSE -

THE CREDIT TITLES

2. <u>THE GREAT CAMP</u> - (NIGHT)

	COOKIE'S VOICE
A wide expanse of barren	(With an occasional
ground checkered with clusters	stammer)

A wide expanse of barren
ground checkered with clusters
of barracks, sectioned off into compounds by double barbed-
wire fences, nine feet high.
Searchlights sweep over the
barracks, the muddy ground
with the snow patches, and the
pine forest beyond the barbed-
wire. The searchlights come
from the goon towers - little
guard houses elevated on poles
- interspersed along the fences.

COOKIE'S VOICE
(With an occasional
stammer)
I don't know about you,
but it always make me
sore when I see those
war pictures - all
about flying leather-
necks and submarine
patrols and frogmen
and guerillas in the
Philippines. I don't
want to take anything
away from those guys,
but what gets me is
that there never was
a movie about P.O.W.s

3. <u>OUR COMPOUND</u>

In the foreground the big gate.
Above it a sign: STALAG 17-D.
On both sides of the gate German
guards in heavy coats, rifles
slung over their shoulders. They
stomp about in enormous boots
with high cork soles to keep
warm.

Beyond the gate about eight low
barracks form a U about the
Appell-ground. They are primitive one-story wooden structures
all set up on stilts about two
feet high.

From one of the buildings - the
Administration Building - flies
the swastika. In between the
barracks are the wash latrines.
A road runs through the slushy
compound to the compound beyond.

- about <u>prisoners</u> <u>of</u>
<u>war</u>. Now my name is
Clarence Harvey Cook,
- they call me Cookie.
I was shot down over
Magdeburg, Germany
back in '43. That's
why I stammer a little
once in a while, es-
pecially when I get
excited and I always
get excited when I
talk about Stalag 17.
I spent two and a half
years in Stalag 17.
Stalag is the Kraut
word for prison camp
and number 17 was some-
where near Krems on
the Danube. There
were about forty thou-
sand P.O.W.s there, if

4. ONE OF THE GOON TOWERS

    A couple of German guards up there,
    one at the machine gun, the other
    working the searchlight.

5. THE HUNDEFUEHRER

    A German guard plodding along
    inside the barbed wire with
    four mean mastiffs straining
    at the leash. The light from
    the goon tower grazes over him.

6. ONE OF THE BARRACKS

    The light sweeps slowly over
    the long shack. Catches the
    sign: BARACKE 4. Catches one
    of the doors, locked from out-
    side with a heavy wooden bar.

7. INSIDE BARRACK 4

    Bunks on both sides. Triple-
    decked bunks. In the bunks
    seventy-five American P.O.W.s
    huddled in blankets. In between
    the bunks, in the little space
    left to them, crude tables, an
    iron stove, makeshift stools.
    Every inch crowded with whatever
    they have. Up above and all the
    way down the barrack hangs their
    wash. Over all of it, the heavy
    stench of seventy-five men cooped
    up. From outside through the
    broken, patched windows the
    searchlight sweeps over the
    bunks. The men are all asleep.
    Or are they?

you bothered to count
the Russians and the
Poles and the Czechs.
In our Compound there
were about six hundred
and thirty of us --
all American airmen,
all shot down by the
Krauts --
radio operators,
gunners and engineers
-- all sergeants.
Now you put six hundred
and thirty sergeants
together and boinnnnng!
-- you've got your-
self a situation!
There was more fire-
works shooting off
around that place!
Take for instance
the story about the spy
we had in our barrack.
It was about a week be-
fore Christmas in '44
and two of our guys --
Manfredi and Johnson
to be exact -- were
just getting set to
blow the joint......

8. THE FAR END OF THE BARRACK

    This is the strategic spot of the story. In the five
    tiers of bunks live our major characters.

    In the upper bunk lies HOFFY. Little fellow. Plenty of
    authority. The Barrack Chief. His eyes are wide open.
    He is studying his wristwatch, the phosphorescent numerals
    shining in the dark.

    In the other bunks lie the others, wide awake, tense:

DUKE, big bellyacher.

TRIZ, six-foot-three, ninety-eight pounds.

PRICE, the barrack Security Chief. Quiet, touch of class.

MANFREDI, no cover, fully dressed.

HARRY, bug-eyed, cocky.

BLONDIE, fair-skinned, boyish.

JOHNSON, fully dressed like Manfredi. Scared.

SEFTON, casual. In his mouth a cold cigar butt.

Hoffy again. Still staring at the wristwatch. This
is the moment. He lifts the metal dogtags off his
chest and jiggles them. This is the signal.

Duke instantly slides out of the bunk, grabs up his
blanket and moves toward the window. A searchlight
beam sweeps across. Duke goes flush on the ground.
The light passes on. Duke gets up again and starts
hanging the blanket over the window.

Now the others go into action, silently, efficiently.
Except for Manfredi and Johnson they are all in long
winter underwear, some in slacks and socks.

As for Sefton, he is lying in his bunk just watching them.

Blondie hangs a blanket over the window. Triz swings
one over the clothesline to shield off their end of the
barrack.

Hoffy and Price light a couple of handmade lamps:
margarine in tin cans with the wick stuck inside.

Manfredi and Johnson are putting on their leather jackets.

Harry tries to awaken STOSH in the bunk above him. The
wooden boards around Stosh's bunk are plastered with
Betty Grable cheesecake. Harry pokes him. Stosh does
not respond. Harry interlocks his fingers, puts them
close to Stosh's ears and cracks them in a SHARP SALVO.
Stosh opens his eyes, dazed. Harry pats Stosh's cheek.

                    HARRY
               (in a whisper)
          Get up, Animal! Betty Grable's
          on the phone!

Stosh gives him a dirty look. Gets out of the bunk.
He and Harry move to the little iron stove. Triz
is already dismantling the pipe above the stove.
Harry and Stosh lift the stove and start inching it
to one side.

Hoffy moving to a large bucket of water. It is a
trick job: a bucket within a bucket. He lifts out
the shallow inner part with the water. Hidden underneath are some civilian clothes. He takes them out,
crosses to Manfredi and Johnson. (All the dialogue
in this scene in whispers, of course.)

> HOFFY
> Here's your civilian clothes, boys.

> MANFREDI
> Okay, Hoffy.

Duke takes the clothes from Hoffy and starts stuffing
them into a small barrack bag.

> HOFFY
> Bury your Army outfits before
> you get out of the forest.

> MANFREDI
> Okay.

> HOFFY
> The compass is the top button
> on your pants, Johnson.

> JOHNSON
> Okay.

Sefton, propped up in his bunk, watches the proceedings with a pitying little smile. He eyes wander to--

Harry and Stosh. By now they have moved the stove
some four feet to the side, and start carefully
lifting some sawed-off planks out of the floor.

Blondie is standing watch by the blanket-covered
window, peeking out.

Price slips a wire hook down into the crack between
a bunk and the wall, fishes out a sheaf of papers
and walks to Manfredi and Johnson.

> PRICE
> Anybody asks for your papers,
> you're French laborers.

He hands them the papers.

                    PRICE
Your map -- your Kraut money --
Swiss francs.

                    MANFREDI
Roger.

                    PRICE
Now, let's hear it once more, boys.

                    JOHNSON
We've been over it a hundred times.

                    HOFFY
Let's hear it again.

                    MANFREDI
We stick to the forest going west
until we hit the Danube -

                    PRICE
Check.

                    JOHNSON
Then follow the Danube up to Linz -

                    PRICE
Check.

                    JOHNSON
In Linz we hop a barge and go all
the way to Ulm -

From OFF come the WEIRD SOUNDS of an ocarina being
played. They turn.

It's JOEY in his bunk playing the sweet potato. He's
nuts all right.

                    DUKE
Stop it, Joey - go to sleep!

Joey hides the ocarina behind his back, afraid they
may take it away.

                    PRICE
                 (To Johnson)
Go on. You're in Ulm.

                    JOHNSON
Once in Ulm we lie low until night,
then take a train to Friedrichshafen.

                    MANFREDI
          Then once in Friedrichshafen we
          steal a rowboat, get some fishing
          tackle, and start drifting across
          the lake -- always south -- until
          we hit the other side -- Switzerland.

Sefton has gotten out of his bunk, and is picking up
the margarine lamp.

                    SEFTON
          Bingo. Once in Switzerland, just give
          out with a big yodel so we'll know
          you're there. It's a breeze, boys.

He lights his cigar butt with the margarine lamp.
Manfredi and Johnson shoot him a nervous glance.

                    HOFFY
          Stay out of it, Sefton.

                    SEFTON
          Just one question. Did you calculate
          the risk?

Harry and Stosh have by now removed the loose planks
off the floor. A small black hole gapes below them.

                    HARRY
          Ready.

Hoffy, Price, Manfredi and Johnson move toward the trap
door, Johnson carrying the barrack bag. Hoffy looks at
his watch.

                    HOFFY
          You got ten minutes to get through the
          tunnel. That'll bring you out just
          when the Jerries are changing shifts.
               (Turns to window)
          Blondie?

Blondie gives him the high sign.

                    HOFFY
               (To Manfredi and Johnson)
          Okay, boys - peel off.

There are handshakes, goodbyes and good-lucks.

                    STOSH
          When you get going on those broads,
          think of me!

                    HARRY
          Animal! Animal! Aren't you ashamed of
          yourself? A couple of guys are trying
          to escape and you're thinking of broads.
          Broads?

He does a take.

                            JOHNSON
                          (With feeling)
                    We'll miss you, you cruds.

He turns and climbs down through the trap. Before
Manfredi follows him, he turns away, goes down on
his knee, crosses himself quickly.

9.   UNDERNEATH BARRACK 4 - (NIGHT)

        Johnson has already landed on the ground. Manfredi
        slips down. They look around and start crawling off
        in the direction of the latrine.

10.   INT. BARRACK 4 - (SHOOTING UP THROUGH TRAP)

        Stosh is peering after them, his head hanging down
        through the trap from above. Beyond him in the
        barrack, Hoffy, Price and Duke bend over Stosh,
        waiting for developments.

11.   UNDERNEATH BARRACK 4 - (NIGHT)

        From Stosh's point of view: Manfredi and Johnson have
        now reached the end of the barrack and are crawling
        into the compound towards the wash latrine some fifteen
        feet away. A searchlight sweeps dangerously towards
        them.

12.   INT. BARRACK 4

        Stosh pulls up from the trap, his eyes closed, his
        fingers in his ears. He doesn't want to see or hear
        the two out there get shot. The others stand petri-
        fied. No shots, no screams. So Stosh bends down
        into the trap again.

13.   EXT. BARRACK 4 - (NIGHT)

        Manfredi and Johnson just manage to fling themselves
        back under the barrack as the searchlight sweeps past.
        Then, they get on their feet again and dash to the
        wash latrine - just ahead of another searchlight from
        the other direction.

14.   INT. WASH LATRINE - (NIGHT)

        A primitive, roofless structure, with wooden partitions
        shielding it from the outside. Above, a water tank
        with pipes running down to spigots over a trough.
        Under the trough, a wooden lattice to stand on.

Manfredi and Johnson have reached first base.
They stand breathless.   Then Manfredi picks up
the lattice, leans it against the trough, and lifts
a dirt-covered trap leading into the tunnel. Johnson
has tied the barrack bag to his own ankle.   They
HEAR BARKING. Freeze.

15.   THE HUNDEFUEHRER

Leading the mastiffs past the wash latrine. One of
the mastiffs is BARKING. He seems to smell something, but the other dogs pull him along.

16.   INT. WASH LATRINE - (NIGHT)

Manfredi and Johnson wait until the BARKING fades
in the distance. Johnson, the barrack bag tied to
his ankle, jumps down into the narrow vertical shaft.
Manfredi follows. He pulls the trap shut over his
head in such a way that the lattice falls into place
on top of it.

17.   THE TUNNEL

A shaft about three feet square and five feet deep
leads into a narrow, crudely shored-up tunnel.
Johnson and Manfredi light their Zippo lighters
and start worming their way through the tunnel,
Johnson leading the way, the barrack bag dragging
from his ankle.

18.   INT. BARRACK 4

Harry and Stosh moving the stove back into place.
Hoffy fixing up the trick bucket. Price pacing up
and down. Sefton leaning against a bunk, smoking
the cigar.

                    HOFFY
          They ought to be under the barbed
          wire soon.

                    BLONDIE
               (still covering the window)
          Looks good outside.

                    STOSH
          I hope they hit the Danube before dawn.

                    PRICE
          They got a good chance. This is
          the longest night of the year.

                    TRIZ
          I bet you they make it to Fried-
          richshafen all right.

                    STOSH
          I bet they get all the way to
          Switzerland!

                    SEFTON
          And I bet they don't even get out
          of the forest.

They all look at him.

                    DUKE
          Now what kind of a crack is that?

                    SEFTON
          No crack. Two packs of cigarettes
          say they don't get out of the forest.

                    HOFFY
          That's enough, Sefton. Crawl back
          into your sack.

                    HARRY
          He'd make book on his own mother
          getting hit by a truck!

Sefton takes two packs of cigarettes from his pocket
and throws them on the table.

                    SEFTON
          Anybody call?

                    HOFFY
          Go on, Sefton - butt out!

                    DUKE
          Wait a minute, Hoffy - I want to
          back those kids. I'll cover ten
          of that.

He starts shaking cigarettes out of his pack onto
the table.

                    TRIZ
          I'll take five.

                    PRICE
          Eight.

                    HOFFY
          Put me down for ten, you louse.

                    DUKE
                (Throwing two packs
                 on the table)
            I'll call the whole pot.

                    SEFTON
            Whatever you say.
                (Calling off)
            Hey, Cookie - get me some more
            cigarettes.

COOKIE, a chipmunk of a kid, scrambles down from his
bunk - the one above Sefton's. Drags out a footlocker
from under Sefton's bunk. The footlocker is chained
to the bunk-post. Cookie opens it, starts taking
cigarettes out.

About twelve guys are around Sefton by now, making
their bets.

                    HARRY
            Here's two and a half.

                    SEFTON
            No butts.

Cookie comes over with a carton.

                    COOKIE
                (With a stammer)
            W-w-will that do or do you want
            some m-m-m -- ?

                    SEFTON
            That'll do.

He rips open the carton.

                    SEFTON
            Speak up, boys. Any more sports
            in the crowd?

19.   INSIDE TUNNEL

       Johnson and Manfredi crawling on, by the light of
       their Zippos. Johnson dragging the bag behind him.
       They are dripping with perspiration. From above
       comes a little shower of loose earth.

       Johnson stops as he comes to the end of the tunnel.
       There is another shaft leading up. He picks up a
       rusty can and starts digging at the earth above.

1-30-52

20. <u>THE OPEN GROUND ABOVE</u> - (NIGHT)

In the pine forest some thirty feet outside the barbed
wire. From the goon towers, the lights sweep over the
camp and over the edge of the forest.

The tin can thrusts through the ground as Johnson digs
into the open. Then, when the opening is wide enough, he
climbs out, his face covered with **sweat** and dirt. He
helps Manfredi out. They lie on the ground for a moment,
exhausted. Then Johnson starts untieing the bag from
his ankle.

> MANFREDI
> Let's go.

He rises. There is a SHARP BURST of MACHINE GUN FIRE.
Manfredi falls instantly. Johnson, not knowing where
the gunfire is coming from, tries to turn and run, the
bag dragging behind him.

From a hillock about thirty feet off a MACHINE GUN,
manned by three German guards, is blasting away.

A light from one of the goon towers picks up Johnson,
running. The machine gun gets him, ripping his chest.
He spins and crumples to the ground. The light swings
to Manfredi. Bleeding, he tries to crawl back to the
safety of the tunnel. There is another BURST of FIRE -

21. <u>INSIDE BARRACK 4</u>

The men have all run to the window and look out.

All except Sefton and Cookie. They stand at the table
where the cigarettes are. And in back of them: Joey,
sitting in his bunk, comprehending nothing.

There is another BURST of FIRE. Then all is silent.
The men turn back into the room, sickened.

> BLONDIE
> Filthy Krauts!

> DUKE
> What slipped up, Hoffy?

> HOFFY
> Don't ask me. **Price was elected Security.**

> DUKE
> (to Price)
> Okay, Security - what happened?

>   PRICE
> I wish I knew. We had everything
> figured out. To the last detail.

>   STOSH
> Maybe the Krauts knew about that
> tunnel all the time!

>   HARRY
> Shut up, Animal!

>   STOSH
> Maybe they were layin' for 'em
> out there!

>   SEFTON
>   (Casually)
> Yeah. Maybe.

He gives Cookie a sign. Cookie pulls the front of his
shirt out of his pants and holds it out against the edge
of the table. Sefton sweeps the mass of cigarettes into
Cookie's shirt.

>   DUKE
> Hold it, Sefton. So we heard some
> shots -- so who says they didn't
> get away?

>   SEFTON
> Anybody here wanna double their bet?

No answer. He nods to Cookie again. Cookie carries the
cigarettes to their bunks. Sefton follows him, kicks
open the footlocker. Cookie dumps the loot in.

The men are looking at them. Stosh sees a cigarette on
the floor which Cookie has dropped. He picks it up and
tosses it into Sefton's footlocker viciously.

FADE OUT

          END OF SEQUENCE A

SEQUENCE B

FADE IN:

22. THE CAMP - DAWN

Another miserable day has begun. The barracks loom in the murky light.

From the Administration Building - the one with the swastika - come a dozen German guards, Lugers hanging from their belts. They spread out and cross the muddy compound toward the barracks, BLOWING WHISTLES shrilly. They lift the wooden bars off the doors and go inside.

FELDWEBEL SCHULZ has arrived at Barrack 4. He is an enormous man, about fifty-five. His cauliflower ears make a good vegetable for his pig-knuckle face. He removes the bar, opens the door, stands there WHISTLING like a madman, enters.

COOKIE'S VOICE
Funny thing about those Krauts. They hated the sight of us yet they couldn't wait to look at us again. Every morning -- at six on the dot -- they'd have the Appell -- that's roll call to you. Each barrack had its own alarm clock. Our alarm clock was Johann Sebastian Schulz. I understand the Krauts had a composer way back with the Johann Sebastian in it -- but I can tell you one thing: Schulz was no composer. He was a Schweinehund. Oh, Mother -- was he ever a lousy Schweinehund!

23. INT. BARRACK 4

Schulz is marching down the barrack, beating the bunks with his stick.

             SCHULZ
    Aufstehen, gentlemen! Appell!
    Raus! Hurry up!

Men start sliding out of their bunks. Others roll over in their sacks, groaning.

             SCHULZ
    You must get up for roll call!
    Raus, raus, gentlemen! Everybody
    aufstehen! Raus!

             MEN
    We heard you, Schulz!
    And good morning to you!
    Aw, break it off!
    Why don't you take that whistle and
        shove it!
    Tell the Kommandant I've got dysentery!

1-30-52

                    MEN (Cont'd)
         Shut up, Schulz -- you're talking
            to sergeants of the United States
            Air Force!
         Look at this chilblain. Ain't it
            a beaut!

                    SCHULZ
         Raus! Raus! Aufstehen!

Whacking the bunks, Schulz has reached our end of
barrack. Hoffy and Price are getting into their
clothes.

                    HOFFY
         Come on, sack rats -- cut the
         bitchin' and get up!

Duke, Triz and Blondie start climbing out, yawning and
scratching themselves.

                    PRICE
         Say, Schulz -- you guys had machine
         gun practice last night?

                    SCHULZ
            (Throwing up his hands)
         Ach, terrible! Such foolish boys.
         Such nice boys. I'd better not
         talk about it. It makes me sick to
         my stomach.

                    DUKE
         You killed them, huh? Both of them?

                    SCHULZ
         Such nice boys! It makes me sick
         to --

                    DUKE
         Don't wear it out!

Schulz moves to Joey. Joey is sitting in his bunk,
TOOTLING on his ocarina. Schulz raps the sweet
potato with his stick.

                    SCHULZ
         Outside! You, too! Put away the
         piccolo!

Joey hides the sweet potato, staring at Schulz,
frightened. Schulz jerks him off the bunk.

1-31-52

                                    SCHULZ
                         Los, los. Dummkopf!

                                    HOFFY
                                (pushing in)
                         Lay off, Schulz. He's got
                         a sickness. He's krank.

                                    SCHULZ
                         Sometimes I think he is fooling
                         us with that crazy business.

                                    HOFFY
                         Yeah? How would you like to see
                         the guts of nine pals splattered
                         all over your plane?
                                (to Joey)
                         C'mon Joey -- don't be afraid.

He helps him up and starts putting clothes on him.

Schultz has approached bunk with Harry and Stosh.
He pokes Harry with the stick.

                                    SCHULZ
                         Aufstehen, gentlemen! Please! You
                         do not want to stay in bed on such
                         a beautiful morning we are having
                         today!

                                    HARRY
                         Say, Schulz --

                                    SCHULZ
                         Jawohl?

                                    HARRY
                         Sprechen Sie deutsch?

                                    SCHULZ
                         Jawohl.

                                    HARRY
                         Then droppen Sie dead!

                                    SCHULZ
                                (splitting his sides)
                         Ja -- ja! Droppen Sie dead! Always
                         mit the jokes! Droppen Sie dead!

He pokes Stosh with the stick.

                                    SCHULZ
                         Aufstehen! Appell!

He moves on.

1-30-52

23

Harry bends over Stosh, shaking him.

> HARRY
> Get up, Animal. Come on!

Stosh doesn't budge. Harry again gives him a knuckle-
cracking salvo. Stosh opens his eyes automatically.

> HARRY
> (sweetly)
> Good morning, Animal! What'll it be
> for breakfast? Scrambled eggs with
> little sausages? Bacon and eggs
> sunny-side up? Griddle cakes? A
> waffle?

> STOSH
> Stop it, Harry!

> HARRY
> Coffee? Milk? Or how about a
> little cocoa?

> STOSH
> (grabbing him by the
> collar)
> Why do you do this to me every
> morning?

> HARRY
> (with sadistic speed)
> Hamburger and onions! Strawberry
> shortcake! Gefillte fish! Banana
> split! French fried potatoes!
> Chicken a la king!

The last items are coming out with a gurgling SOUND
as Stosh tightens the grip on Harry's neck.

> STOSH
> I'll kill you, Harry - so help me!

> HARRY
> Let go, Animal! It's roll call!
> Hitler wants to see you!

Sefton is standing near his bunk, getting dressed.
Cookie is helping him to zip up his luxurious
flyer's boots.

> SCHULZ
> Good morning, Sefton.

> SEFTON
> Good morning, Schulz. And how's
> Mrs. Schulz? And all the little
> Schulzes?

1-30-52

              SCHULZ
    Fine - fine!

He looks at the two bunks which were occupied by
Manfredi and Johnson. Takes off his gloves.

              SCHULZ
    Let us see. We have now two
    empty bunks here.
              (Takes out pencil and
              notebook, writes)
    Nummer einundsiebzig und Nummer
    dreiundsiebzig in Baracke vier.

              PRICE
    Suppose you let those mattresses
    cool off a little - just out of
    decency?

              SCHULZ
    Ja, ja, gewiss! It is only that
    we are cramped for space with new
    prisoners every day.
              (To the whole barrack)
    Gentlemen! Outside! Please!
    Do you want me to have trouble with
    the Kommandant again!

He starts herding them out the door.

              STOSH
    Hey, Schulz -- as long as you're
    going to move somebody in - how
    about a couple of those Russian
    broads?

              SCHULZ
    Russian women prisoners?

              HARRY
    Jawohl!

              SCHULZ
    Some are not bad at all.

              STOSH
    Just get us a couple with big
    Glockenspiels.

              SCHULZ
    Ja! Ja! Droppen Sie dead!

Splitting his sides, he pushes them out, and follows.

25

EXT. COMPOUND - COLD GREY MORNING

Most of the P.O.W.s are out of their barracks by now.
A mass of freezing, disheveled men. Some wear Army
coats over their underwear, knitted caps pulled down
over their ears. Some are huddled in blankets, their
feet in wooden clogs. Only a few are fully dressed
and shaven. A few are on crutches or bandaged up.

They assemble before their respective barracks, form-
ing a U facing the center of the compound. The barrack
chiefs are assisting the guards in lining them up,
fifteen abreast and five deep.

Supervised by Schulz and Hoffy the last ones from
Barrack 4 emerge.

                    HOFFY
        All right, men -- fall in!

From OFF comes:

                    GERMAN OFFICER'S VOICE
            Ach - tung! Abzaehlen!

The HUB-BUB dies down.

The guards march down the front line of their barrack
groups, counting the lines of five in German.

As Schulz passes him, Blondie spots something in the
middle of the compound. He nudges Duke. Duke nudges
Price, Price Harry, Harry Stosh, Stosh Cookie. Cookie
nudges Sefton who is putting on his wool gloves. The
glove drops. They all look off in the same direction.

In the center of the compound, right smack in the mud,
lie the corpses of Johnson and Manfredi, covered with
a blanket. You know it's them because Johnson's foot
is sticking out, with the barrack bag still tied to it.

A stir goes through the men of Barrack 4. They are
hit hard. All but Sefton. He looks at the corpses
for a moment, then bends down, picks up the glove and
starts putting it on.

In front of the Administration Building a German
Lieutenant has been supervising a couple of guards
as they lay narrow planks over the mud in a line
leading to the middle of the compound. He turns now
to the P.O.W.s.

                    GERMAN LIEUTENANT
        Parade Atten-tion!

The German guards come to rigid attention.   The
Americans just stand there, sullenly.

The Lieutenant comes to a heil salute.   Through the
open door of the Administration Building steps the
Kommandant, OBERST VON SCHERBACH, followed by another
Lieutenant. Von Scherbach is a big erect officer of
the Potsdam School.   Over his shoulder hangs a fur-
lined officer's coat.   His boots shine like polished.
glass.   He glances over the compound, then walks down
the planks, followed by the two Lieutenants, marching
through the mud on both sides of him.   Von Scherbach
stops at the end of the plank.   In front of him lies
a deep puddle.   He clicks his heels and raises his
hand in a heil salute.

>   VON SCHERBACH
>   Guten Morgen, Sergeants!

A glowering silence from the men.   Von Scherbach
lowers his hand.

>   VON SCHERBACH
>   Nasty weather we're having, eh?
>   And I so much hoped that we could
>   give you a white Christmas -- just
>   like the ones you used to know ...
>   Aren't those the words that clever
>   little man wrote -- you know the
>   one who stole his name from our
>   capital -- that something-or-other
>   Berlin?

He waits until his nasty little joke sinks in.
Schulz has come up to the Lieutenant, salutes and
hands him the slips of paper with the prisoner count.

>   VON SCHERBACH
>   Look at that mud.   Come spring --
>   and I do hope you'll still be with
>   us next spring -- we shall plant
>   some grass here -- and perhaps
>   some daffodils --

He turns to the Lieutenant for the tabulations.

>   VON SCHERBACH
>   Ich bitte!

>   LIEUTENANT
>   (Checking the papers)
>   Melde gehorchsamst: 628 Gefangene.
>   Zwei Mann fehlen in Baracke vier.

                         VON SCHERBACH
                      (To the P.O.W.s)
                  I understand we are minus two men
                  this morning. I am surprised at you,
                  gentlemen. Here I am trying to be
                  your friend and you do these embarrass-
                  ing things to me. Don't you know this
                  could get me into hot water with the
                  High Command? They do not like men
                  escaping from Stalag 17 - especially,
                  not enemy airmen from Compound D. We
                  plucked you out of the skies and now
                  we must see to it you do not fly away.
                  Because you would come back and blast
                  our cities again. The High Command
                  would be very angry with me. They would
                  strip me of my rank. They would court-
                  martial me, after all these years of a
                  perfect record! Now you wouldn't want
                  that to happen to me, would you?
                  Fortunately, those two men --

From the ranks of the men comes the EERIE DISSONANT
SOUNDS of Joey's SWEET POTATO.

Joey, in the second row of the Barrack 4 company, is
playing on his ocarina, oblivious to what is going on.
Stosh turns and quickly grabs the ocarina from Joey's
mouth.

Von Scherbach chooses to disregard the little musical
interlude.

                         VON SCHERBACH
                  As I was saying: fortunately those
                  two men did not get very far. They
                  had the good sense to rejoin us again,
                  so my record would stand unblemished.
                  Nobody has ever escaped from Stalag 17.
                  Not alive, anyway.

He snaps his fingers in the direction of the guard
who stands watch over the corpses.

The guard pulls back the blanket in such a manner that
all we can see is the barrack bag tied to Johnson's
leg.

The P.O.W.s however see the corpses. There is an
ANGRY BUZZ.

Hoffy marches up to Von Scherbach.

                         HOFFY
                      (saluting)
                  Sergeant Hoffman from Barrack 4.

                              VON SCHERBACH
                    Yes, Sergeant Hoffman?

                              HOFFY
                    As the duly elected Compound Chief,
                    I protest the way these bodies are
                    left lying in the mud.

                              VON SCHERBACH
                    Anything else?

                              HOFFY
                    Yes. According to the Geneva Con-
                    vention, dead prisoners are to be
                    given a decent burial.

                              VON SCHERBACH
                    Of course. I'm aware of the Geneva
                    Convention. They will be given the
                    burial they deserve. Or perhaps you
                    would suggest we haul in twenty-one
                    cannons from the Eastern Front and
                    give them a twenty-one gun salute?

          Hoffy turns on his heel and walks back to his men.

          Von Scherbach, without even looking at the corpses,
          snaps his fingers. The guard throws the blanket
          back over the bodies.

                              VON SCHERBACH
                    For the last time, gentlemen, let me
                    remind you: any prisoners found out-
                    side the barracks after lights out will
                    be shot on sight. Furthermore, the
                    iron stove in Barrack 4, the one
                    camouflaging the trap door, will be
                    removed. And so that the men from
                    this barrack will not suffer from the
                    cold, they will keep warm by filling
                    in the escape tunnel. Is that clear?

          The men just stand there, in frustrated anger. Stosh
          clenches the ocarina in his fist.

                              VON SCHERBACH
                    All right, then, gentlemen. We are
                    all friends again. And with Christ-
                    mas coming on, I have a special treat
                    for you. I'll have you all deloused
                    for the holidays. And I'll have a
                    little tree for every barrack. You
                    will like that.

          Stosh, with a quick underhand flip, throws the sweet
          potato in the direction of Von Scherbach.

1-30-52

It lands smack in the middle of the puddle in front
of Von Scherbach and splashes his boots with mud.

>   VON SCHERBACH
>   (stiffening)
>   Who did this?

Absolute silence.

>   VON SCHERBACH
>   I will give the funny man exactly
>   five seconds to step forward.

He looks about the compound. Five seconds pass.
Nobody moves.

>   VON SCHERBACH
>   Then you shall all stand here if it
>   takes all day and all night.

From the ranks of the men of Barrack 4, Stosh steps
forward.

>   VON SCHERBACH
>   That is better!

But his triumph is short-lived, for almost instantly
Harry steps forward alongside Stosh. Then Duke and
Blondie and Cookie. Spontaneously, men from all the
other barracks follow until all the P.O.W.s have
moved forward one step.

>   VON SCHERBACH
>   I see! Six hundred funny men! ...
>   There will be no Christmas trees!
>   But there will be delousing.
>   (to Schulz)
>   With ice water from the hoses!

He wheels about and marches back up the plank and
into the Administration Building. His Lieutenants
after him. Two of the guards start picking up the
planks again.

>   SCHULZ
>   (shouting, to the P.O.W.s)
>   Dismissed!

The men break ranks, going off in all directions,
some back to the barracks, some toward the latrines.

Only Joey stands where he stood, his eyes fastened on
the puddle. Slowly he walks toward it. He bends
down and fishes out his sweet potato, dripping with
mud. It is broken. He wipes the pieces off on his
coat and hides them inside his jacket.

1-20-52

25.   INT. WASH LATRINE

Packed with men from Barrack 4, about two dozen of
them. Others waiting outside for their turn. At the
trough washing: Hoffy, Price, Duke, Stosh, Harry,
Cookie and Sefton. No soap. A couple of worn-out
towels. Except for Sefton: He's got soap, towel and
tooth brush.

                    STOSH
            (Imitating von Scherbach)
        'We will remove the iron stove --
        the one that was camouflaging the
        trap door.'

                    HARRY
        I'm telling you, Animal, these
        Nazis ain't Kosher.

                    STOSH
        You can say that again!

                    HARRY
        I'm telling you, Animal - these
        Nazis ain't Ko --

                    STOSH
            (Grabbing him)
        I said say it again. I didn't
        say repeat it.

Triz reaches for Sefton's soap, but gets a sharp rap
on the knuckles.

                    SEFTON
        Private property, bub.

                    DUKE
        How come the Krauts knew about
        that stove, Security? And the tunnel?
        How come you can't lay down a belch
        around here without them knowing it?

                    PRICE
        Look -- if you don't like the way
        I'm handling this job --

                    HOFFY
        Kill it, Duke. It's got us all
        spinning.

                    DUKE
        I just want to know what makes those
        Krauts so smart.

                    STOSH
        Maybe they're doin' it with radar.
        Maybe they got a mike hidden some
        place.
                    HARRY
        Yeah. Right up Joey's ocarina.

1-30-52

> DUKE
> Or maybe it's not that they're so
> smart. Maybe it's that we're so
> stupid. Maybe there's somebody
> in our barracks that's tipping
> 'em off! One of us!

> HOFFY
> Come again?

> DUKE
> You betcha. I said one of us is a
> stoolie. A dirty, stinkin' stoolie!

> SEFTON
> Is that Einstein's theory? Or did
> you figure it out yourself?

A P.O.W. sticks his head into the doorway.

> P.O.W.
> (Breathless)
> New dames in the Russian compound!

Stosh lets go with a SCREAM. He takes off like shot
from a cannon, Harry after him. Instantly the wash
latrine is emptied of the men, wet as they are.
Nobody is left but Price, Hoffy, Duke, Sefton and
Cookie.

26.   EXT. COMPOUND

It's a stampede. P.O.W.s are rushing across the
compound toward the Russian compound.

Stosh, charging like a bull, gets tripped and falls
flat on his puss right into a mud puddle. Harry zooms
past him. Stosh picks himself up and runs after him,
his winter underwear dripping with mud.

27.   THE BARBED WIRE FENCE

dividing the American and Russian compounds. P.O.W.s
rush in from all sides, about a hundred of them. They
go as far as they are permitted; to a low warning wire,
running parallel to the big fence some fifteen feet
away. To cross the warning wire is verboten. The
German guards up in the goon towers insure that.

There is great excitement among the P.O.W.s. Some give
out with cat-calls and wolf-whistles; others just
stand there staring.

Beyond the fence a new batch of Russian prisoners has just been brought in. German guards are counting some sixty prisoners, about twenty of them women. They all are in uniforms and wear boots, a bedraggled lot. The women are big buxom dames, not exactly Golden Circle material, but this is war.

The Americans jump up and down trying to attract the women's attention. They throw cigarettes, chewing gum, chocolate. One guy is dancing the Kazatski, two of his pals holding him up.

                    P.O.W.s
          Yee-ow!
          Tovarich! Tovarich!
          Oh you sweethearts!
          Let's open the third front!
          Hey, Minsk - Pinsk!
          How about some borscht -- the two of us!

Stosh and Harry push right up to trip wire. Stosh, plastered with mud, goes completely berserk.

                    STOSH
          Hey -- Russki -- Russki! Look at
          those bublichkis! Over here!

                    HARRY
          Comrade! Comrade! Otchi Tchorniya --
          Otchi Tchorniya!

Stosh puts two fingers in his mouth and tries to whistle. He gets his mouth full of mud. Spits out the mud. Searches madly through his pockets and throws whatever he can find across the fence.

                    STOSH
          Chewing gum -- chewing gum!

Some of the Russian women break the ranks to pick up the goodies that come flying over. The German guards push them back. The women smile at the Americans and wave.

                    STOSH
               (At the top of his lungs)
          Look at me! I'm your baby!
               (To Harry)
          Get a load of that blonde one!
          Built like a brick Kremlin!

                    HARRY
          Hey -- Comrade! Over here! This is
          Harry Shapiro -- the Volga Boatman
          of Barrack four!

                    STOSH
          Lay off! The blonde is mine!

The women are being led away by the guards.

1-30-52

33

                              STOSH
                            (Screaming)
                    Hey, Olga -- Volga -- wait for
                    me!

He takes off blindly toward the women, trips immediately over the warning wire and falls flat on his
face in the mud again.

Up in the goon tower the guard swivels the machine
gun and yells down.

                              GUARD
                    Zurueck oder wir schiessen!
                    Zurueck!

Harry frantically grabs Stosh by the feet and pulls
him back, under the wire.

                              STOSH
                    Let me go! Let me go!

                              HARRY
                    They'll shoot you, Animal!

He lies right on top of him, holding him by the
wrists.

                              STOSH
                    I don't care! Let me go!

From OFF come the SOUNDS of a dishpan being beaten
and shouts of "Chow!" Some of the P.O.W.s start to
go back to the barracks.

                              HARRY
                    It's chow, Animal! Chow!

                              STOSH
                    Who wants to eat? I just
                    wanna get over there!

                              HARRY
                    No you don't! You don't want
                    any broads with boots on!

                              STOSH
                    I don't care if they wear
                    galoshes!

                              HARRY
                    You want Betty Grable!

1-30-52

                    STOSH
          Let me go!

                    HARRY
               (Yelling)
          Betty Grable!

Stosh's face lights up.

                    HARRY
          Animal! When the war's over,
          remember I told you I'd fix you
          up with Betty Grable!

                    STOSH
          Yeah? How you going to fix me
          up with Betty Grable?

                    HARRY
          How? We go to California. I got
          a cousin that's working for the
          Los Angeles Gas Company. That's
          how we get the address, see? Isn't
          that clever? I take you up to her
          house and ring the doorbell and say,
          'Congratulations, Miss Grable. We
          have voted you the girl we'd most
          like to be behind barbed wire with,
          and I'm here to present the award'.

                    STOSH
          What's the award?

                    HARRY
          What d'ya think, jerko! You're
          the award!

                    STOSH
          Me? What if she don't want me?

                    HARRY
          If she don't want you, she don't
          get anything.

                    STOSH
               (Grabbing him)
          You're teasing me again!

                    HARRY
               (Gagging)
          Let go, Animal! It's chow! We'll
          miss chow!

Stosh relaxes his hold and drops him like a limp rag.
They scramble to their feet and run off towards
Barrack 4.

1-30-52

28.   INT. BARRACK 4

Chow time. Most of the men sit around eating. Only
a few are still in line. They stand before a washtub,
from which Triz ladles out a thin brew. Then each man
gets a pitiful slice of sawdust bread, cut by Blondie
at the table.

                    1ST G.I.
                 (In chow line)
        What's this stuff anyhow? Manicure
        water?

                    2ND G.I.
        This is what I like -- a hearty
        meal.

                    3RD G.I.
        They finally found the formula: an
        Ersatz of an Ersatz.

Hoffy, back in the line with Joey, carrying both chow
cans.

                    HOFFY
        What's holding up the parade?

                    4TH G.I.
        Are you supposed to drink this
        stuff or shave?

                    DUKE
                 (Next in line)
        Drink.
                 (Tastes the stuff)
        Shave.

Hoffy gets the two cans filled, gives one to Joey.
This is the end of the line.

                    TRIZ
        Anyone else want potato soup?

No answer. He takes out a homemade washboard and a
pair of socks, puts them in the tea and starts scrub-
bing.

Through the door, Stosh and Harry come running.

                    STOSH
                 (Out of breath)
        Chow! Where's the chow!

He dashes to his bunk, gets his chow can and is about
to dip it into the tub, when he sees what Triz is
doing.

                        STOSH
            Take your socks outa my breakfast!

Triz takes the socks out. Stosh dips in his chow can.

                        HARRY
            No, Animal.   .

                        STOSH
            No?

                        HARRY
            No. Your eyeball goes. The top of
            your head. Gotta wind up with
            athlete's stomach.

Stosh pours back his tea, a miserable man. His eyes
fall on the door. An electric shock goes through him.
He grabs Harry's arm. They look off:

Sefton has come into the barrack and is crossing toward
the iron stove. In his hand is the incredible -- more
beautiful than all the Kohinoors in the world: an egg.

Harry and Stosh stand there with their eyes bulging.
They start forward, drawn by the egg.

Cookie is at the stove, tending a can of boiling water.
He sees Sefton and puts a makeshift skillet (the banged-
up top of a tin can) with a dab of margarine in it, on
the fire. Sefton takes some keys out of his pocket,
tosses them to Cookie.

                        SEFTON
            Set 'er up, Cookie. I'm starved.

Cookie goes towards Sefton's bunk. Sefton cracks the
egg into the skillet. Stosh and Harry move in, their
eyes bulging at sight of the sizzling beauty.

                        HARRY
            Easy, Animal! Easy!

                        STOSH
            Where'd that come from?

                        SEFTON
            From a chicken, bug-wit.

                        STOSH
            A chicken?

                        HARRY
            Don't you remember, Animal? A
            chicken lays those things.

                        STOSH
            It's beautiful!

37

                              STOSH (Cont'd)
                           (To Sefton)
                    You goin' to eat it all yourself?

                              SEFTON
                    Uh-huh. The yellow and the white.

He flips the egg over in the skillet. Harry and Stosh
cover their eyes and yelp in panic. To their relief
they see that the egg has landed safely. The aroma of
the frying egg has brought about six P.O.W.s down from
their bunks. They crowd around, their mouths watering.

                              STOSH
                    Is it all right if we smell it?

                              SHEFTON
                    Just don't drool on it.

                              HARRY
                    You're not going to eat the eggshells?

                              SEFTON
                    Help yourself.

He tosses him the eggshells. Harry gives one half to
Stosh.

                              STOSH
                           (Grateful)
                    Thanks. You're a real pal!
                           (On second thought)
                    What're we goin' to do with it?

                              HARRY
                    Plant it, Animal, and grow us a
                    chicken for Christmas.

Cookie, at Sefton's bunk, has taken from one of the
footlockers three cans, a china cup with a broken
handle, a fork, a spoon, and a salt-and-pepper shaker.
He slams the locker shut with his foot and sets everything up on the other footlocker. Hoffy, Duke and
Price, seated at the table eating chow, eye him with
disgust.

From the stove comes Sefton carrying the skillet and
the can of boiling water. The other P.O.W.s, including
Harry and Stosh, follow him, hypnotized by the egg.
Sefton walks to his bunk, sits down on a little stool,
puts salt and pepper on the egg. Cookie meanwhile has
opened the cans. From one of them he measures out a
spoonful of instant coffee into the cup and pours the

1-30-52

boiling water over it. Sefton takes two lumps of
sugar out of the other can and some Zwieback from the
third can. The guys around him sniff the royal breakfast. The situation is tense.

> HOFFY
> If I were you, Sefton, I'd eat that
> egg some place else. Like for in-
> stance under the barrack.

> SEFTON
> (Sipping the coffee,
>   to Cookie)
> A little weak today.

Cookie puts another half a spoonful of instant
coffee into the cup.

> DUKE
> Come on, Trader Horn! Let's
> hear it: what'd you give the
> Krauts for that egg?

> SEFTON
> (Eating away)
> Forty-five cigarettes. The
> price has gone up.

> STOSH
> That wouldn't be the cigarettes
> you took us for last night?

> SEFTON
> What was I going to do with
> them? I only smoke cigars.

> DUKE
> Nice guy! The Krauts shoot
> Manfredi and Johnson last night
> and today he's out trading with
> them.

> SEFTON
> Look, this may be my last hot
> breakfast on account of they're
> going to take away that stove.
> So will you let me eat it in
> peace?

> STOSH
> Ain't that too bad! Tomorrow
> he'll have to suck a raw egg!

1-30-52

                    HARRY
        He don't have to worry. He'll trade
        the Krauts for a six-burner gas range.
        Maybe a deep freeze too.

                    SEFTON
        What's your beef, boys? So I'm
        trading. Everybody here is trading.
        Only maybe I trade a little sharper.
        So that makes me a collaborator.

                    DUKE
        A lot sharper, Sefton! I'd like to
        have some of that loot you got in
        those footlockers!

                    SEFTON
        You would, would you? Listen, Stupe --
        the first week I was in this joint
        somebody stole my Red Cross package,
        my blanket and my left shoe. Well,
        I wised up since. This ain't no
        Salvation Army -- this is everybody for
        himself. Dog eat dog.

                    DUKE
        You stink, Sefton!

    He goes after him.

                    HOFFY
        Come off it! Both of you!

    A couple of P.O.W.s hold Duke back.

                    SEFTON
        Now you've done it. You've given
        me nervous indigestion.
            (He gets up)
        Anything else bothering you, boys?

                    PRICE
        Just one little thing. How come
        you were so sure Manfredi and
        Johnson wouldn't get out of the
        forest?

                    SEFTON
        I wasn't so sure. I just liked the
        odds.

    He picks up the skillet with the half-eaten egg.

                    SEFTON
        And what's that crack supposed to
        mean?

PRICE
They're lying dead in the mud out
there and I'm trying to find out how
come.

SEFTON
I'll tell you how come.
(Pointing at Hoffy)
The Barrack Chief gave them the
green light. And you, our Security
Officer, said it'd be safe. That's
how come.

He crosses to Joey who has been sitting on the edge
of the bunk looking on blankly and puts the skillet
with the egg on his lap. Turns back to the others.

SEFTON
What're you guys trying to prove
anyway? Cutting trap doors! Digging
tunnels! You know what the chances are
to get out of here? And let's say you
do get all the way to Switzerland! Or
say to the States? So what? They ship
you to the Pacific and slap you in
another plane. And you get shot down
again and you wind **up in a Japanese prison**
camp. That's if you're lucky! Well,
I'm no escape artist! You can be the
heroes, the boys with the fruit salad
on your chest. Me -- I'm staying put.
And I'm going to make myself as com-
fortable as I can. And if it takes a
little trading with the enemy to get me
some food or a better mattress or a
woman -- that's okay by Sefton!

He strikes a match on the sleeve of Duke's leather
jacket and lights himself a cigar.

DUKE
Why you crud! This war's going to be
over some day - then what do you think
we'll do to Kraut-kissers like you?

He lunges forward and there is a fracas, the others
trying to hold them back.

From OFF comes:

MARKO'S VOICE
At ease! At ease!

MARKO, the Inter-barrack Communications officer, has
entered from the compound, followed by a one-legged
P.O.W., THE CRUTCH. Marko gets up on a stool a piece
of paper in his hand.

MARKO
(Yelling)
AT EASE!

                    HOFFY
          Break it off, boys! At ease for
          the news!

The ruckus subsides.

                    MARKO
          Today's Camp News!
              (Reading)
          Father Murray announces that due to
          local regulations the Christmas mid-
          night Mass will be held at seven in
          the morning!

                    STOSH
          You can tell Father Murray to --

                    MARKO
          At ease! He also says, quote:
          All you sack rats better show up for
          the services and no bull from anybody.
          Unquote. At ease! Monday afternoon
          a sailboat race will be held at the
          cesspool. See Oscar Rudolph of Bar-
          rack 7 if you want to enter a yacht.
          Next: Jack Cushingham and Larry Blake
          will play Frank deNotta and Mike Cohen
          for the pinochle championship of the
          camp.

                    HARRY
          That's a fix.

                    MARKO
          At ease! Tuesday afternoon at two
          o'clock all men from Texas will meet
          behind the north latrine.

Boos and cheers.

                    MARKO
          At ease! Next: A warning from
          Kommandant von Scherbach. Anybody
          found throwing rocks at low-flying
          German aircraft will be thrown in
          the boob. At ease! At ease!
              (Then in a lower voice)
          Are the doors covered?

He looks around to make sure.

                    MARKO
              (To The Crutch)
          Okay, Steve. Give 'em the radio.

The Crutch, leaning against the edge of the table,
pulls up the empty pant leg. Attached there is a
small radio, a makeshift set with tubes showing.
Also a pair of earphones. Blondie starts getting
it out.

                    MARKO
                 (To Hoffy)
          You can keep it for two days.

                    HOFFY
          Two days? We're supposed to
          have it for a week!

                    MARKO
          You're lucky to get it at all. The
          boys are afraid the Jerries'll find
          it here. This barrack is jinxed.

                    PRICE
          Don't worry. We'll take care of it.

                    HOFFY
                 (To Stosh and Harry)
          Take some men and get the antenna
          going. Let's see if we can catch
          the BBC.

In the background, Harry gets a volley ball from
under the bunk, Stosh picks up a roll of chicken wire
from a corner of the barrack, and the two lead six
other P.O.W.s out into the compound.

                    MARKO
          What about those guys last night?
          What gives in this barrack anyway?

                    DUKE
          Just a little sickness. Somebody
          around here's got the German measles.

                    SEFTON
          He oughta know. He went to Johns
          Hopkins. He used to be a bedpan.

                    MARKO
          What's the gag?

                    SEFTON
                 (Imitating him)
          At ease!   At ease!

Marko shrugs and turns to Hoffy.

                            MARKO
                Be sure to put down the news.
                Looks like the Germans have
                started a counter-offensive and
                the other barracks want to know.

Marko and The Crutch go off.

29.   EXT. BARRACK 4

The men are setting up the chicken wire, attaching
one end to the barrack, and the other to a tall post:
it becomes a volley ball net, and in turn, an antenna.
Stosh is slipping a wire through the window into the
barrack. They divide into two teams, Stosh and Harry
on opposite sides, and start playing volley ball. In
the background, Marko and The Crutch are seen walking
away.

30.   INT. BARRACK 4

Triz has connected the antenna wire to the radio on
the t able. Blondie is sitting there with the earphones on, working the dials, Price sitting next to
him with pencil and paper. The others stand around
waiting.

                        PRICE
                Getting anything?

                        BLONDIE
                Getting too much. I'm tryin'
                to unscramble.

                        SEFTON
                If you can't get the BBC, how about
                getting Guy Lombardo?

                        HOFFY
                Are we boring you?

                        BLONDIE
                Hold it...Quiet...

He repeats what he hears over the earphones while
Price writes it down.

                        BLONDIE
                ...has driven across Luxemburg...The
                second German wedge is reported fourteen
                miles west of Malmedy where tank columns
                cut the road to Bastogne...the Allied
                Air Force is grounded by poor visibility...

The boys don't like what they hear.

31.   EXT. BARRACK 4

The volley ball game is in fine progress, the ball
popping back and forth across the antenna. A German
guard approaches, puzzled over the sports activity
on this lousy winter day. He is a singularly grim
fellow. He starts circling them. Harry and Stosh,
to appear nonchalant, break into the SCHNITZELBANK
SONG. The guard moves dangerously close to the
window. Quickly Harry flips the ball over the net at
him. The guard slaps it back across the net. Again
Harry pops it at him ... and slowly the guard finds
himself sucked into the game.

                    HARRY
          Wunderbar! Isn't he wunderbar!

                    STOSH
          He's the grrrrreatest!

The guard permits himself a smile as he goes on playing.

32.   INT. BARRACK 4

The boys around the radio.

                    BLONDIE
               (Repeating what he hears)
          ... five Panzer divisions and nine
          infantry divisions of von Rundstedt's
          army have poured into the wide breach ...
          meanwhile two of Patton's tank units
          have been diverted toward Bastogne and
          are trying to --

It's jammed again. Blondie fiddles with the dials.

                    HOFFY
          Come on!

                    BLONDIE
          Static!

                    DUKE
          Static is right! The radio's static,
          Patton's static, we're static!

                    SEFTON
          Maybe it's going to be a longer war
          than you figured - eh, Duke?

Triz, who has been standing watch at the door, now
sees:

33.   EXT. COMPOUND

Marching toward Barrack 4 are four German soldiers
headed by Schulz.

34.   INT. BARRACK 4

Triz reaches up and snaps a string. All the wash in
the barrack jumps up and down. That's the signal.

Immediately the boys jump into action. Triz and
Blondie disconnect the wires. Hoffy takes the radio
off the table and they all start dispersing.

35.   EXT. BARRACK 4

Schulz and the four German soldiers are about to
enter the barrack. Schulz pauses as he sees the
guard playing volley ball enthusiastically. Schulz
taps him on his back. The guard wheels around,
freezes, clicks his heels. Schulz gives him a dis-
approving look. Then he leads the four soldiers
into the barrack. Harry, Stosh and the other P.O.W.s
follow, worried.

Schulz and the soldiers enter the barrack, followed
by Harry, Stosh and the other players.

The guys have just assumed innocent positions. A
little too innocent maybe.

                    SCHULZ
          Did I interrupt something, gentlemen?

                    STOSH
          Yeah. We were just passing out guns.

                    SCHULZ
               (Laughing)
          Always joking. Always making wise-
          crackers!

                    HARRY
          Wisecrackers? Where did he pick up
          his English? In a pretzel factory?

                    SCHULZ
          You always think I am a square. I
          have been to America.
               (He shows them his
                cauliflower ears)
          I wrestled in Milwaukee and St. Louis
          and Cincinnati. And I will go back!
          The way the war is going I will be
          there before you!

                        HARRY
        You should live so long.

Schulz has taken a wallet out of his pocket, shows a
photograph to them.

                        SCHULZ
        This is me in Cincinnati.

                        STOSH
        Who's the other wrestler? The one with
        the mustache?

                        SCHULZ
        That is my wife.

                        STOSH
                (Taking the photograph)
        Look at all that meat. Isn't she the
        bitter end!

                        SCHULZ
                (Snatching it from him)
        Give it back. You must not arouse
        yourselves.

                        HARRY
        Hey, Schulz! I got a deal for you.
        Suppose you help us escape. We'll go
        home and have everything ready for you
        in Madison Square Garden. For the world
        championship! Schulz, the Beast of
        Bavaria versus Halitosis Jones!

                        SCHULZ
        Droppen Sie dead!
                (To the German soldiers)
        Raus mit dem Ofen. Los! Los!

The soldiers move toward the stove. As the scene
proceeds they dismantle the stove and ultimately
carry it out.

                        SCHULZ
                (To the P.O.W.s)
        All right, gentlemen! We will now all
        go outside for a little gymnastic and
        take some shovels and undig the tunnel
        which you digged.

                        STOSH
        Why don't we just plug up that tunnel -
        with the Kommandant on one end and you
        on the other.

SCHULZ
It is not me. It is the orders. I
am your friend. I am your best
friend here.

DUKE
Cut out the guff, Schulz. We're on
to you. You know everything that's
happening in this barrack. Who's
tipping you off?

SCHULZ
Tipping me off? I do not understand.

HOFFY
You're wasting your time, Duke.
          (To the others)
Outside, everybody! Let's get it
over with.

PRICE
Wait a second, Hoffy. Schulz says
he's our best friend. Maybe he can
give us a little hint.

DUKE
Come on, Schulz! Spill it! How did
you get the information? About Manfredi
and Johnson? About the stove and the
tunnel? Who's giving it to you? Which
one of us is it?

SCHULZ
Which one of you is what?

PRICE
Which one of us is the informer?

SCHULZ
You are trying to say that an American
would inform on other Americans?

DUKE
That's the general idea.
          (Looking at Sefton)
Only it's not so general as far as
I'm concerned.

SCHULZ
You are talking crazy!

SEFTON
          (Taking the cigar out
          of his mouth)
No use, Schulz. You might as well come
clean. Why don't you just tell 'em it's
me. Because I'm really the illegitimate
son of Hitler. And after the Germans
win the war you'll make me the Gauleiter
of Zinzinnati.

                    SHULZ
          You Americans! You are the craziest
          people! That's why I like you! I
          wish I could invite you all to my
          house for a nice German Christmas!

                    HARRY
                (To Stosh)
          Why don't we accept, Animal? The
          worst that can happen is we wind up
          a couple of lamp shades.

                    SHULZ
                (Jovially)
          Raus! Raus! All of you!

By this time most of them have put on their warm clothes,
caps and gloves and are filing out.

Schulz starts to follow them, but stops short as he sees:

The electric light bulb hanging by a wire from the ceiling.
Just the bulb. No shade. The wire is tied up into a slip
knot.

Schulz reacts to what he has seen. He watches the last of
the P.O.W.s leave, and the Germans carry the stove out of
the barrack. He closes the door. His entire attitude has
changed. He is serious and efficient. He walks over to
the chess set on the table. Out of his pocket he takes a
chess piece - a black queen - and exchanges it with the
black queen from the set. He puts it in his pocket.
Steps over to the light bulb, pulls the slip knot free and
exits.

The light bulb hangs straight now, swaying gently in the empty barrack.	COOKIE'S VOICE He was the Beast of Bavaria all right, as we pieced it together later. And there was a stoolie in our barrack, just as Duke said. They had a very simple communications system - Schulz and the stoolie...

36. <u>EXT. COMPOUND</u>

The men from Barrack 4 are lined up between the latrine and the barbed wire, starting to dig up the tunnel. They are supervised by German guards. In the background, Schulz is crossing from the barrack towards the Administration Building. As the men dig, they look off at:	That's how the Krauts knew about the tunnel, from the day we started digging. Those poor suckers Manfredi and Johnson! They got out of Stalag 17 sure enough, only not quite the way they wanted to go.
An open German half-truck driving toward the big gate, carrying two crude wooden coffins.	

The men have stopped dig-
ging. As the CAMERA goes
down the row they take off
their caps. Joey does not
comprehend. Blondie, standing next to him, takes the cap
off for him. The CAMERA PULLS
PAST Cookie who has taken his
cap off, and now STOPS on
Sefton. He has seen the cof-
fins. He has seen the others
take off their caps. He takes
the cigar out of his mouth,
snuffs it out, puts it into
his pocket, and slowly
pulls off his cap.

As for the stoolie, I just wish he
had German measles because when you
get the measles you break out all
over in red spots, and we could
have pegged him easy. As it was it
could have been anybody in our out-
fit - Duke or Hoffy or Price or
Goofy Joey or Harry or the Animal
or maybe Sefton. Sergeant J. J.
Sefton. I guess it's about time
I told you a few more things about
that Sefton guy. If I was anything
of a writer I'd send it in to the
Reader's Digest for one of those
'Most Unforgettable Characters
You've Ever Met'....

DISSOLVE:

END OF SEQUENCE B

SEQUENCE C

37.   EXT. COMPOUND - (DAY)

A circle about 15 feet in diameter is drawn on the barren ground with white lime. Around it, some forty G.I.s. In the center, Cookie, holding a cardboard box. To one side, standing on a wooden crate, Sefton. In front of him, a makeshift bookie's desk, a heap of loose cigarettes on top. G.I.s are crowding around, making wagers in cigarettes. Hanging off one side of the desk, the odds board:

NO.	HORSE	ODDS
1.	Whirlaway	3:1
2.	Seabiscuit	5:1
3.	Equipoise	1:1
4.	Twenty Grand	4:1
5.	Schnickelfritz	10:1

COOKIE'S VOICE

...he was a B.T.O., Sefton was. A Big Time Operator. Always hustling, always scrounging. Take for instance the horse races. Every Saturday and Sunday he would put on horse races. He was the sole owner and operator of the Stalag 17 Turf Club. He was the Presiding Steward, the Chief Handicapper, the Starter, the Judge, the Breeder and his own bookie. He was the whole works, except that I was the stable boy for ten smokes a day.

                    SEFTON
Step up, boys! The horses
are at the post!

                    G.I.s
Five on Equipoise!
Give me Equipoise - ten on the nose!
Two on Twenty Grand!
Schnickelfritz for me. Five smackers!
Equipoise - one solid pack!

            LAST G.I. (An unkempt bum)
Five on Seabiscuit! Pay you when
the Red Cross parcels come in.

                    SEFTON
No credit.

                    UNKEMPT BUM
Have a heart, Sefton!

                    SEFTON
Sorry. It's against the rules of
the Racing Commission.
        (Calling out)
Already? Any more bets? Shake
'em up, Cookie!

1-30-52

Cookie shakes the cardboard box, puts it face down on the ground in the center of the circle.

> SEFTON
> Let 'er go! They're off and
> running at Stalag 17!

Cookie has lifted the box. There are five mice of various colors with numbers 1 to 5 attached to their backs. The mice start spreading hesitantly in all directions.

The P.O.W.s YELL and SCREAM, rooting for their horses to reach the circle line first.

Among the P.O.W.s Stosh and Harry. Stosh, with a bundle of mutuel tickets in his hand, screaming his head off.

> STOSH
> Equipoise! Oh, you beauty! This
> way! This way!

Equipoise, No. 3, pulls in front and is only a few feet from the edge of the circle.

> HARRY
> Equipoise! Equipoise! What did
> I tell you, Animal?

> STOSH
> Come on, baby! Daddy's going to
> buy you a hunk of cheese!

Equipoise, now only a foot from the finish line, suddenly stops and goes into a dizzy spin. The other mice gain rapidly.

> STOSH AND HARRY
> Straighten out, you dog!
> This way!
> That's no horse - that's a dervish!
> Please! This way! Come to Daddy!

In a turmoil of SCREAMING G.I.s, Schnickelfritz passes Equipoise, still spinning like a top, and crosses the line.

> SEFTON
> The winner is No. 5: Schnickelfritz!

Stosh grabs Harry.

> STOSH
> Schnickelfritz! I told you
> Schnickelfritz! Why'd you
> make me bet on Equipoise!

445.

                    HARRY
          I clocked him this morning. He
          was running like a doll.

                    STOSH
                 (Choking him)
          You clocked him! Why don't I
          clock you?

                    SEFTON
                 (Calling out)
          The next race will be a claiming
          race for four months old and up-
          ward which have not won since
          November 17th.

                                        COOKIE'S VOICE
While Sefton pays off the   It's a good thing nobody
winners, Cookie puts up   ever asked for a saliva
a new odds board. New   test. Because I wouldn't
bettors start lining up   have put it past Sefton
on the other side.   to stiff a horse once in
Among them, Harry and   a while - especially when
Stosh.   the betting was heavy.

DISSOLVE:

38.   <u>INT. BARRACK 4</u> - (DAY)

                                        COOKIE'S VOICE
Near Sefton's bunk, the dis-   Another one of his enter-
tillery is set up: a Rube   prises was the distil-
Goldberg contraption of old   lery. Believe it or not,
tin cans and a maze of piping, he ran a bar right in
a margarine lamp burning un-   our barrack, selling
der the boiler. The whole   Schnapps at two cigarettes
thing SPUTTERS and HISSES.   a shot. The boys called
                               it the Flamethrower,
Behind a makeshift wooden   but it wasn't really
shelf - the bar - stands   that bad. We brewed
Cookie, pouring drinks for   it out of old potato
some eight customers, among   peels and once in a
them Harry and Stosh,   while a couple of
crocked. In Stosh's hand is   strings off the Red Cross
the big Betty Grable cheese-   parcels, to give it a
cake photo from his bunk.   little flavor.

                    STOSH
                 (In a crying jag)
          It's not fair, Harry. I'm telling
          you, it's not fair! She's been
          married for over a year! My Betty!
          She had a baby! Didn't you hear
          it on the radio!

53

                    HARRY
          C'mon, Animal! Pull yourself
          together!
                (Off)
          Hey, Cookie! Belt us again!

He pushes their little condensed milk cans, serving
as jiggers, across the bar, counts out four cigarettes.

                    STOSH
          Look at her! Isn't she beauti-
          ful! Married an orchestra leader!

                    HARRY
          So what? There's other women!

                    STOSH
          Not for me! Betty! Betty!

                    HARRY
          Cut it out, Animal! I'll fix
          you up with a couple of those
          Russian women!

                    STOSH
                (Sarcastically)
          You'll fix me up!

                    HARRY
          Sure, Animal! I'll get you
          over there!

                    STOSH
          How? Pinky Miller from Barrack
          8 tried to get over there and
          they shot him in the leg!

                    HARRY
          It takes a gimmick, Animal, and
          I figured us a little gimmick.

                    STOCK
          You did?

                    HARRY
                (Tapping his forehead)
          Sharp. Sometimes I'm so sharp
          it's frightening.

Cookie slides over the two tin jiggers. Harry picks
them up, hands one to Stosh.

                    HARRY
                (Toasting)
          To the Brick Kremlin!

                    STOSH
            (His eyes on the cheese-
             cake photo)
        She'll never forgive me!

                    HARRY
        Bombs away!

They both drink it down in one gulp, Harry holding
his nose. It's terrible stuff and hits them hard.
Stosh goes into a violent fit of coughing, pulling
his barrack cap down over his eyes.

                    HARRY
            (To Cookie)
        What are you serving today?
        Nitric acid?

                    COOKIE
        I only work here. Talk to the
        Management.

He points to Sefton, who is taking inventory of the
cigarettes in his footlocker: cartons, packages,
loose ones. He is tabulating the amounts on a piece
of paper.

                    HARRY
        All right, Management. What
        are you trying to do? Embalm
        us while we're alive?

                    SEFTON
        Exactly what did you expect for
        two cigarettes? Eight year old
        Bottled-In-Bond? All the house
        guarantees is that you don't go
        blind.
            (To Cookie)
        Don't ever serve 'em again.

                    STOSH
        Blind! Harry! Harry!

He staggers around, not realizing his cap is pulled
down over his eyes.

                    STOSH
        Harry - I'm blind!

                    HARRY
            (Pushing up his cap)
        Blind? How stupid can you get,
        Animal? I drank the stuff
        myself.

1-30-52

Suddenly he seems not to see too well himself. He
gropes around in panic.

> HARRY
> Animal! Animal! Where are you,
> Animal?

DISSOLVE:

39.   INT. BARRACK 4 - (DAY)

A big telescope, about seven
feet long, is set up on a tri-
pod at the window pointing
toward the Russian Compound.
The telescope is made of
various-sized cans soldered
together. It's run by Cookie,
behind a table, piled with
cigarettes and chocolate bars.
Bent down peering through the
telescope, panning it slowly,
is a P.O.W. Across the barrack stretches a long line
of impatient customers, all
the way to the open door and
out of it. Cookie taps the
peeker to indicate his time
is up. The next in line pays
his cigarette and peeks

COOKIE'S VOICE
The killer-diller, of
course - the real
bonanza - was when Sefton
put up the Observatory.
He scrounged himself
some high-powered Kraut
lenses and a magnifying
mirror and got Ronnie
Bigelow from Barrack 2
to put the whole
shebang together for
a pound of coffee.
On a clear day you
could have seen the
Swiss Alps, only who
wanted to see the Swiss
Alps? It was about
a mile away, that Rus-
sian delousing shack,
but we were right on
top of it. It cost
you a cigarette or
a half bar of
chocolate a peek. You
couldn't catch much
through that steam, but
believe you me, after
two years in that camp
just the idea what was
behind that steam sure
spruced up your voltage.

40.   RUSSIAN DELOUSING SHACK -
        (THROUGH THE TELESCOPE)

About a dozen Russian women,
wrapped only in blankets,
waiting in line. The telescope pans across a couple
of windows. They are completely steamed-up by the
disinfecting vapors.

41.   INT. BARRACK 4

The P.O.W. is glued to the telescope. Cookie taps
him on the shoulder.

> COOKIE
> Let's go! Thirty seconds to a
> customer.

Without moving his eye from the telescope, the P.O.W.
fishes another cigarette from his pocket and gives it
to Cookie.

Sefton stands at the open barrack door, a cold cigar
in his mouth. He surveys the landoffice business,
both inside and out, for beyond him a line of about
forty more P.O.W.s stretches into the compound.

                         P.O.W.
                    (From rear of line)
                 Hey, Sefton - what's snarling
                 up the traffic? By the time we
                 get to look they'll be old hags!

                         SEFTON
                 Simmer down, boys. There'll be
                 a second show when they put the
                 next batch through.

Hoffy, Price and Duke come in from the compound.
Hoffy cases the situation and pulls Sefton to the
side.

                         HOFFY
                 What's the big idea, Sefton? Take
                 that telescope out of here.

                         SEFTON
                 Says who?

                         HOFFY
                 Says me.

                         SEFTON
                 You take it out. Only you're
                 going to have a riot on your hands.

                         HOFFY
                 Every time the men get Red Cross
                 packages you have to think up an
                 angle to rob them.

                         PRICE
                 When the Krauts find that gadget
                 they'll throw us all in the boob.

                         SEFTON
                 They know about that gadget. I'd
                 worry more about the radio.

                         DUKE
                 I suppose they also know about your
                 distillery and the horseraces?

                         SEFTON
                 That's right.

                         DUKE
                 Just what makes you and them
                 Krauts so buddy-buddy?

1-30-52

57

                    SEFTON
          Ask Security.
               (To Price)
          You tell him, Price. You've got
          me shadowed every minute of the
          day. Or haven't you found out yet?

                    PRICE
          Not yet.

                    HOFFY
          Answer the question. How do you
          rate all those privileges?

                    SEFTON
          I grease the Kraut guards. With
          ten percent of the take.

                    DUKE
          And maybe a little something else?

                    SEFTON
          A little something what?

He strikes a match on Duke's dogtag and lights his
cigar.

                    DUKE
               (Lunging at him)
          Maybe a little information!

Hoffy and Price hold back Duke.

                    HOFFY
          Break it off!

                    DUKE
          How much more do we have to take
          from him?

                    HOFFY
          There'll be no vigilante stuff.
          Not while I'm Barrack Chief.

From the window come excited shouts.

                    G. I. VOICES
          Hey, look at them!
          It's Harry and the Animal!
          Look what they're doing!

Everybody in the barrack is dashing toward the
window giving out on the Russian Compound. Hoffy,
Price, Duke, and Sefton follow after.

The window is packed by G.I.s staring out. More
crowding in.

> G.I.s
> Those crazy jerks!
> They won't get away with it!
> The Krauts will shoot them!

42.   EXT. COMPOUND - (DAY)

This is Harry's little gimmick: He and Stosh are
painting a white line down the middle of the road
leading towards the Russian Compound. Stosh carries
the bucket and Harry, moving backwards, wields the
brush. They are very close now to the barbed wire
fence dividing the compounds. A bespectacled
German guard is standing in front of his sentinel
house.

They crouch as low as they can as they paint themselves through the gate past the guard and up the
road toward the Russian delousing shack. The guard
gives them a glance. It looks okay to him. He
starts stamping about at the open gate.

43.   INT. BARRACK 4

G.I.s at the window, watching in great excitement.

> G.I.s
> They're past the fifty yard line!
> Quarterback sneak!
> Look at them go!

> SIX G.I.s
> (In chorus)
> We want a touchdown! We want a
> touchdown! We want a touchdown!

> HOFFY
> Those idiots! They'll paint
> themselves into their graves!

44.   EXT. RUSSIAN COMPOUND

Harry and Stosh are doing dandy as they paint up
the highway. Harry gets his bearings: the delousing shack is some twenty-five feet off the road. He
paints a very elegant turn off the highway.

45.   THE GATE BETWEEN THE COMPOUNDS

The German guard is stamping up and down. Suddenly
he does a double take as he sees:

1-30-52

46. EXT. RUSSIAN COMPOUND

The white line leading down the middle of the highway
veers off idiotically over the terrain towards the
shack.

47. THE GERMAN GUARD

He stands there perplexed, then takes off after them.

48. EXT. DELOUSING SHACK

Harry and Stosh have now painted up to the window of
the shack. Without even stopping, they paint right
up the wall and around the window. As they paint,
they peer in through the thick steam (through which
we cannot distinguish anything). Now, they paint
down the building on the other side of the window and
toward the doorway. Into their pathway come the boots
of the German guard. They paint right over the boots.
Then they see the butt of the guard's rifle. They
look at each other. They are in trouble. They stop
painting and straighten up slowly.

                    GERMAN GUARD
              Was ist denn hier los? Sie
              sind verhaftet!

Harry gives the guard's eye-glasses a couple of quick
strokes of paint. Dropping paint and brush, Stosh
and he run like mad back toward the gate.

The guard stands there struggling with his glasses.
The Russian women, huddled in blankets, giggle their
heads off.

FADE OUT.

              END OF SEQUENCE C

SEQUENCE D

FADE IN:

49.   INT. BARRACK 4 - (DAY)   COOKIE'S VOICE

About twenty P.O.W.s lazing   Now let me see,
about. The sack rats in their   what came next?
bunks. Triz and Price playing   Oh, yes. Next
chess, Joey looking on blankly.   came those new
Sefton, a towel around his neck,   prisoners. 'Twas
is sitting in a chair being   two days before
shaved by Cookie. Stosh, in his   Christmas when all
bunk, is carving a new ocarina   through the camp,
for Joey out of wood. CAMERA   not a creature was
MOVES SLOWLY to: stirring, not even
                                       that lamp.
The electric light bulb, hanging
straight and innocent on its wire.

                    MARKO'S VOICE
         At ease!   At ease!

Marko, carrying a handful of letters and a book, has
entered, followed by The Crutch.

                    MARKO
         Mail call!   .

The whole barrack springs to life, everyone moving
towards Marko with whistles, screams and hoorays.
Joey, who keeps staring at the chess board. Sefton
and Cookie go on with the shave.

                    MARKO
         At ease! At ease! First, the
         Kommandant is sending every barrack
         a little Christmas present. A copy
         of Mein Kampf. In the words of
         Oberst von Scherbach: 'Now that a
         German victory is in sight, all
         American prisoners are to be indoc-
         trinated with the teachings of der
         Fuehrer. Unquote. In my own words:
              (He lets go
               with a belch)
         Unquote.

He tosses the book into the air. Duke catches it.

                    DUKE
         That's the wrong direction.

He flings it at Sefton. It sails past Sefton's head.
Cookie ducks. Sefton doesn't even bat an eyelash.

1-30-52

                              SEFTON
              You must have been some tail gunner!
                   (To Cookie)
              Go ahead, Cookie.

                              STOSH
              Come on, let's get that mail.
              Anything for Stanislaus Kuzawa?

                              MARKO
              At ease! At ease!

As Marko calls out the names he hands out the letters.
Some of the men open them immediately. Others go to
their bunks to read.

                              MARKO
              Martin. Shapiro. Price. Trzcinski.
              McKay. Shapiro. Shapiro. Manfredi.

There is an awkward pause, then Marko puts Manfredi's
letter in his pocket.

                              MARKO
              Shapiro. Musgrove. McKay. Peterson.
              Cook.

Cookie comes up for his letter. So do Duke and
Blondie. (Their names are Musgrove and Peterson.)

                              MARKO
              Pirelli. Coleman. Agnew. Shapiro.

                              STOSH
                   (In a little voice)
              Nothing for Kuzawa?

                              MARKO
              Shapiro. Shapiro.

                              STOSH
                   (To Harry)
              Just what makes you so popular?

                              HARRY
                   (Fanning the letters)
              Frightening, isn't it? Fifty million
              guys floating around back home and all
              those dames want is Sugar-lips Shapiro.

                              MARKO
              McKay, Agnew. Here, Stosh.

He holds out a letter.

1-30-52

                    STOSH
                 (Revitalized)
          Yeah?

                    MARKO
          Give this to Joey, will you?

                    STOSH
          Oh.

Marko has now distributed all the letters.

                    MARKO
          At ease! At ease! Here's a
          little something from Father
          Murray. One to each barrack.

He has knelt down in front of The Crutch and pulls
out from the empty pant's leg a little Christmas
tree.

                    MARKO
          And he says he wants you cruds
          to cut out all swearing during
          Yuletide.

                    G.I.
          How'd he get those trees?

                    MARKO
          I don't know. Prayed, I guess.
          They grew out of his mattress.

Marko sticks the tree into one of the margarine cans.

                    G.I.
          What'll we use for decorations?

                    MARKO
          For that you got to pray yourself.

He goes, followed by The Crutch.

Stosh sits next to Joey at the table, reading his
letter to him.

                    STOSH
          '... and we do hope that you will
          finish that last year of law school
          when you come back home...'
                 (Looks up at Joey)
          Law school?! You don't want to
          be a stinking lawyer with a stinking
          brief case in a stinking office, do
          you, Joey?

Joey just sits there. Stosh goes on reading.

                    STOSH
        '...And do keep writing, son.
        Your letters are very dear to us.
        With all our love, Dad.' Here,
        Joey, take it.

Joey doesn't move.

                    STOSH
        It's from your Dad, Joey.

He shoves the letter into Joey's pocket.

                    STOSH
        The next time we write to your
        folks, Joey, you know what you're
        going to say? You're going to say
        you don't want to be a lawyer any
        more. You want to be a musician -
        like play the flute, maybe - eh,
        Joey?

There is a fleeting smile on Joey's face.

Triz, in his bunk, a crumpled letter in his hand, is
mumbling to himself.

                    TRIZ
        I believe it! I believe it!

                    G.I.
        You believe what?

                    TRIZ
        My wife.
            (Reading)
        'Darling, you won't believe it,
        but I found the most adorable
        baby on our doorstep and I have
        decided to keep it for our own.
        Now, you won't believe it, but it's
        got exactly my eyes and nose...'
        Why does she always say I won't
        believe it? I believe it!

Blondie is reading his letter, several G.I.s around
him, among them Duke.

                    BLONDIE
        This is from my mother.
            (He reads)
        'I saw a wonderful article on German
        prison camps in one of the magazines.
        They showed pictures of the tennis
        courts and they also say that in the
        winter they freeze them over so you
        boys can ice skate...'

                              DUKE
          Anything about us grouse hunting
          in the Vienna woods?

                            BLONDIE
                    (Continues to read)
          '...In a way I'm glad you're not
          in America right now - with every-
          thing rationed here, like gas and
          meat.'

                              DUKE
          Heart-rendering, ain't it? Why don't
          we send them some food parcels?

Harry is busy with all his mail. He has opened six
of his letters and is now working on the last. Stosh
comes into the SHOT and peeks over his shoulder.

                            STOSH
          What do those broads say?

                            HARRY
          What do they always say?

                            STOSH
          That's what I wanna hear.

                            HARRY
                    (Hiding the letters)
          It's not good for you, Animal.

Stosh grabs one of the letters from him.

                            STOSH
          Hey! This is with a typewriter!
          It's from a finance company!

                            HARRY
          So it is from the finance company.
          So it's better than no letter at
          all. So they want the third payment
          on the Plymouth.
                    (Showing him
                    five more letters)
          So they want the fourth, the fifth,
          the sixth and the seventh. So they
          want the Plymouth.

                            STOSH
          Sugar-lips Shapiro! Frightening,
          ain't it?

1-30-52

65

                                    HARRY
                            (Holding up the
                            last letter)
                    This is a good one!
                            (Mounts a stool)
                    Shut up, everybody! Listen to
                    this!
                            (He reads)
                    'The President of the United States
                    to Harry Shapiro. Greeting: Having
                    submitted yourself to a local board,
                    you are hereby notified to report...'
                    What do you know! So now I'm a draft
                    evader!

50.   EXT. BARRACK 4 - (DAY)

        Hoffy is walking across the muddy compound towards the
        barrack, leading a couple of new prisoners: LIEUTENANT
        DUNBAR and SERGEANT BAGRADIAN. They are exhausted but,
        by contrast to the old P.O.W.s, remarkably clean.
        They are followed by a P.O.W., carrying two barrack
        bags.

                                    HOFFY
                            (Opening door to
                            barrack)
                    This is it, gentlemen. Don't
                    bother to scrape your shoes.

        He leads them into the barrack.

51.   INT. BARRACK 4

        Hoffy leads in Dunbar, Bagradian and the P.O.W. with
        the barrack bags. He snaps the line, the wash jiggles
        through the barrack. Everybody turns.

                                    HOFFY
                    Okay, gang! Meet our new guests.
                    This is Lieutenant Dunbar and this
                    is Sergeant Bagradian.

                            DUNBAR AND BAGRADIAN
                    Hi.

                                    STOSH
                    Lieutenant?!

        The whole barracks comes to its feet and salutes him
        with mock reverence. Harry dashes up and polishes with
        his sleeve the Lieutenant's bar.

                                    DUNBAR
                    Knock it off, boys. The pleasure's
                    all mine.

1-30-52

HOFFY

The Lieutenant will be with us
for a week or so until the Krauts
can ship him to the officers'
camp in Silesia. Looks like all
the railroad lines out of Frankfurt are fouled up because somebody
blew up an ammunition train.

BAGRADIAN

Somebody, my eye.
(Indicating Dunbar)
The Lieutenant did it - right in
the station - with fifty German
guards around.

HARRY
(Climbing off the
stool)
Well! Glad to have you with the
organization!

STOSH

You're just in time for the
Christmas Pageant.

BAGRADIAN

Looks more like the lost company
of Tobacco Road.

P.O.W. WITH
BARRACK BAGS
(Indicating Bagradian)
He's an actor. You should see
him do imitations. He can
imitate anybody.

HARRY

If he can imitate a girl, he's
made.

P.O.W.

Hey - do Lionel Barrymore.

STOSH

Do Grable.

HOFFY

Stop it, boys. They were shot
down two days ago and they've
been on their feet ever since.
(To Stosh and Harry)
Fix them some tea, will you?
(To Dunbar and Bagradian)
Price will show you your bunks.

Price leads them towards the bunks which were for-
merly occupied by Manfredi and Johnson, the P.O.W.
with the barrack bags following them.

> PRICE
> We had a couple of unexpected
> vacancies. Which one will it be
> - the upper or lower, Lieutenant
> Dunbar?

> DUNBAR
> Doesn't matter.

Cookie is just finished shaving Sefton. Sefton
turns in his chair.

> SEFTON
> Lieutenant Dunbar? It wouldn't
> be James Schuyler Dunbar? From
> Boston?

> DUNBAR
> Yes, it would. Do we know each
> other?

> STOSH
>   (indicating Sefton)
> He's from Boston, too. But you
> wouldn't know him, not unless
> you had your house robbed.

Sefton gets up, wiping the soap off his ears with
the towel.

> SEFTON
> Maybe he would. We applied for
> Officers' Training together,
> remember? They turned me down,
> but I'm glad to see you made it.
> Of course, it couldn't be that
> all that dough behind you had
> something to do with it!
>   (to the others)
> His mother's got twenty million
> dollars.

> DUNBAR
> Twenty-five.

> SEFTON
> They've got a summer house in
> Nantucket, with an upstairs polo
> field.
>   (to Price)
> You better put a canopy over his
> bunk.

> HOFFY
>
> Lay off, Sefton.

> SEFTON
> (To Dunbar)
>
> With your mother's pull, how come
> you're not a chicken colonel by
> now?

> HOFFY
>
> Lay off, I said - if you don't
> want your head handed to you.

> HARRY
> (From the table)
>
> Tea is being served on the
> verandah!

Harry sets two chow cans on the table.

> HARRY
> (To Stosh)
>
> Where are the napkins, Animal?

Stosh tears off two sheets of toilet paper from a
roll, separates them and puts them next to the chow
cans. By now, Dunbar and Bagradian come over to the
table.

> BAGRADIAN
> (To Dunbar, a la
> Ronald Colman)
>
> Do be seated, Bonita. What a
> perfectly charming table
> arrangement. They must have
> copied it from House Beautiful.

Stosh starts pouring hot water from the pot.

> HARRY
>
> Animal! How many times have I
> told you, you got to pour from
> the left!

Stosh reverses his direction. Harry has taken a
faded tea bag out of his watch pocket. He dunks it
three times into each chow can. Then, looking at
the tea bag as if it were a watch:

> HARRY
>
> Dinner will be served at seven
> sharp. Black tie.

He puts the tea bag back into his watch pocket.

> HOFFY
>
> Where'd they get you, Lieutenant?
> Over Frankfurt?

                    DUNBAR
On the Schweinfurt run.

                    HOFFY
How many ships did you lose?

                    DUNBAR
Half the group.

                    PRICE
Flying out of England?

                    DUNBAR
Yes. Paddington, 92nd Bomber
Group.

                    BLONDIE
        (Wide-eyed)
Hey, Lieutenant. How did you
blow up that train with fifty
guards around?

                    DUNBAR
Just lucky, I guess.

                    BAGRADIAN
Don't let him kid you. Cagney
couldn't have pulled a sweeter
job.
        (a la Cagney)
All right, boys. We were waiting
in the depot in Frankfurt, see?
And there was an ammunition train
coming through, the longest ammunition train you ever saw, see? So
Dunbar gets himself in the men's
room, see? Fixes himself a time
bomb, busts open the window and
just as the train moves out, lays
the thing in there, see? So then,
he comes out like nothing's happened
and three minutes later you can
hear it - boom! Broke every window
in Frankfurt. It was gorgeous!

                    HOFFY
I wouldn't talk about things like
that.

                    BAGRADIAN
        (himself again)
They never caught on.

                    HOFFY
They may. That's why I would keep
my mouth shut.

1-30-52

                    DUNBAR
We're all Americans here!

                    PRICE
The Krauts have a way of getting
information.

                    DUKE
Especially in this barrack.

                    DUNBAR
How?

                    PRICE
That's what we'd like to know.

Sefton is just putting on his leather jacket. He has
been listening to what has been going on. Cookie
hands him out of the footlocker a bottle of Rhine
wine and a carton of cigarettes. Sefton tucks them
inside his leather jacket. Cookie now hands him a
pair of silk stockings.

                    COOKIE
                (In a low voice)
There's only one pair left.

                    SEFTON
                (Putting the stockings
                 in his pocket)
We'll get some more.

He puts his cap on and walks toward the door. As he
passes the others:

                    DUNBAR
Where does a guy take a hot
shower around here?

                    STOSH
Hot showers? Dig him!

                    PRICE
Sorry. No hot showers. You
wash in the latrine.

                    DUNBAR
Latrine?

                    SEFTON
                (Stopping in his tracks)
What did you expect, glamor boy?
The Officers' Club with a steam
room and a massage maybe?

1-30-52

71

                    DUNBAR
              (Going after him)
        Just a minute. You made a couple
        of cracks before and I let them
        slide. But I don't intend to
        take any more. If you resent my
        having money, start a revolution,
        but get off my back.

                    SEFTON
        Look, Lieutenant. All your dough
        won't help you here. Because here
        you're on your own. And no mother
        to throw you a lifebelt. Now let's
        see how good you can swim.

He has picked a little twig off the Christmas tree.
He puts it in his buttonhole.

                    SEFTON
        Sorry, boys, but my taxi's waiting.

He goes out.

                    BAGRADIAN
        What's wrong with him?

                    HOFFY
        Plenty.

                    STOSH
        Number one on the rat parade!

Hoffy nods to Duke. Duke leaves the barrack, after
Sefton.

52.   EXT. COMPOUND - (DAY)

       On the muddy compound there is a tag football game
       going on with some forty G.I.s watching.

       Sefton is walking along. Behind him, Duke has come
       out of the barrack and is following him. Sefton
       becomes aware of it. Nonchalantly, he walks into a
       wash latrine.

53.   INT. WASH LATRINE

       Sefton comes in. There is another P.O.W. there, a
       colored guy, just finishing washing his hands. Sefton
       quickly climbs up a couple of rungs of the ladder
       leading to the water tank and stops there. The
       colored P.O.W. doesn't notice it.

54.   <u>EXT. WASH LATRINE</u>

Duke stands some distance away, watching the only
pair of legs visible under the raised partition.
The legs move now **down** the length of the latrine and
out the other end. The colored P.O.W. emerges and
walks off with his back toward Duke. Duke follows
him.

55.   <u>INT. WASH LATRINE</u>

Sefton jumps off the ladder
and exits the way he came in.

56.   <u>EXT. COMPOUND</u>

Duke is still following the
wrong guy. Now the P.O.W.
stops to talk to a pal. Duke
realizes his mistake. He
dashes back into the wash
latrine and comes out again.
He stands there frustrated.
With the football players
rushing about, passes being
thrown and G.I.s milling
around, he has lost Sefton.

DISSOLVE:

57.   <u>INT. BARRACK 4</u> - (DAY)

START on the electric light -
the cord is again <u>tied</u> <u>up</u> <u>into</u>
<u>a noose</u>.

                    COOKIE'S VOICE
              It was a funny thing
              about Sefton and me.
              I guess I knew him as
              well as anybody else in
              the camp because I had
              worked for him for two
              years. But there were
              lots of things I
              didn't know about him.
              Take for instance,
              where he would dis-
              appear to once in
              a while. Of course,
              I had a hunch, but
              it seemed so crazy
              I couldn't quite
              believe it --
              Just as I would
              never have believed
              that Sefton was
              the guy that would
              give away Lieutenant
              Dunbar for blowing up
              that ammunition train.

CAMERA PANS to Harry. He is made up a la Hitler;
his hair is combed across his forehead and a charcoal mustache on his lip. He is now making up Joey
as Hitler, with two fingers blackened in charcoal.
Joey just sits in his bunk, dumbly.

At the table, Hoffy is playing gin with Dunbar. Price
kibitzing.

                    HOFFY
                 (To Harry)
         Cut the horseplay, Harry. What's
         the matter with you **guys**?

                    PRICE
         And don't blame me if you all wind
         up in the cooler.

                    DUNBAR
         How's two?

73

He lays down his hand.

Stosh, at the door, holds it slightly ajar and peeks out into the compound. He too is made up as Hitler.

      STOSH
    Get ready! Here he comes!

He SLAMS the door, snaps wash line.

58. <u>EXT. BARRACK 4</u> - (DAY)

A German truck draws up, loaded with blankets. Schulz, sitting next to the driver, gets out and starts into the barrack. Two German guards stay behind.

59. <u>INT. BARRACK 4</u>

Schulz enters, closes the door behind him. From OFF comes Bagradian's voice: A double-talk German gibberish in the characteristic guttural sounds of der Fuehrer.

Schulz stops, mystified.

Bagradian stands on a stool giving a lecture to some thirty P.O.W.s, all of them with their backs towards Schulz. Bagradian's face cannot be seen as he holds the Mein Kampf book in front of it. Schulz listens for a little while to Bagradian's ranting and raving. Then he stamps his foot.

      SCHULZ
   Gentlemen! Gentlemen! Attention!

- Bagradian lowers the book. He too is made up as Hitler. He raises his arm in the Nazi salute.

      BAGRADIAN
   Heil, Hitler!

      SCHULZ
    (Responding automatically)
   Heil,Hitler!

He catches himself, lowers the arm.

      SCHULZ
    (Jovially)
   Droppen Sie dead.

      BAGRADIAN
    (a la Hitler)
   Quiet! We are indoctrinating!
    (to the others)
1-30-52   Is you all indoctrinated?

                    P.O.W.s
                 (In unison)
          Jawohl.

                    BAGRADIAN
          Is you all good Nazis?

                    P.O.W.s
          Jawohl.

                    BAGRADIAN
          Is you all little Adolfs?

                    P.O.W.s
          Jawohl!

                    BAGRADIAN
          Then we shall all zalute Feldwebel
          von und zu Schulz! About face!

The P.O.W.s wheel around and face Schulz. They are
all made up as Hitler.

                    P.O.W.s
          Sieg heil! Sieg heil! Sieg
          Heil!

After each 'Sieg heil' they raise their arms in salute.

                    SCHULZ
          Ach! One Fuehrer is enough! Now
          please, gentlemen! Take off the
          mustaches immediately. Or do you
          want me arrested by the Gestapo?

                    P.O.W.s
          Jawohl!

                    SCHULZ
          You would be very sorry to get
          a new Feldwebel. Somebody with-
          out a sense of humor.

                    HOFFY
          Okay, boys. Wipe off the
          mustaches. Now what is it,
          Schulz?

The men start wiping off the mustaches and straighten-
ing their hair.

1-30-52

                    SCHULZ
          Gentlemen, tomorrow morning the
          Geneva Man is coming to inspect
          the camp whether we are living up
          to the International Convention.
          I am sure he will find we are
          treating you very well. You must
          not run around in your underwear.
          And take off the wash. The Kom-
          mandant wants all the barracks to
          be spic and also span.

                    STOSH
          We'll put pink ribbons on the bedbugs.

                    SCHULZ
          The Kommandant also sends you
          clean blankets. He wants every
          man to have a new,clean blanket.

                    HOFFY
          We know! We got them last year.
          Five minutes after the Geneva Man
          was gone, the blankets were gone.

                    SCHULZ
          One more thing, gentlemen. The
          Kommandant told me to pick up
          the radio.

                    HOFFY
          What radio?

                    SCHULZ
          The one you are hiding in the
          barrack, don't you know? The
          one your friend without the leg
          is smuggling all over the compound.

                    PRICE
          Schulz, you're off your nut!

                    SCHULZ'
          Give me the radio.

                    PRICE
          We have no radio.

                    SCHULZ
          All right, gentlemen, I will find
          it myself. Now let's see.

          He starts wandering around the barrack, drawing
          closer and closer to the trick bucket.

1-30-52

                    SCHULZ
          Am I cold? Am I getting warmer?
          Hot, maybe? Very hot?

He has reached the bucket. With his boot he kicks
it over on the floor. The water spills on Cookie's
shoes. The radio and the earphones lie on the floor.

                    SCHULZ
                (Picking up radio)
          What is this? This is water?

                    HARRY
          It's a mouse trap.

                    SCHULZ
                (Holding up earphones)
          And this?

                    STOSH
          My grandmother's ear-muffs.

                    SCHULZ
                (To Dunbar)
          Look at them, Lieutenant. Every-
          body is a clown! How do you expect
          to win the war with an army of
          clowns?

                    DUNBAR
          We sort of hope you'll laugh your-
          selves to death.

Schulz gives out with a big phony laugh. As he
laughs his eyes fall on:

The light bulb and the cord tied up in a noose.

Schulz stops laughing.

                    SCHULZ
          Now, outside everybody, for the
          blankets! Everybody out!

He herds them out. Joey is in his bunk, still wear-
ing the Hitler mustache.

                    SCHULZ
          Outside! You, too!

He pushes Joey out. Alone in the barrack again,
Schulz quickly walks to the table, exchanges the
black queens and straightens out the light cord.

60.   EXT. BARRACK 4 - (DAY)

The men, standing in line are being issued new
blankets by the two German guards.

                    HARRY
            That Schulz pig. I'll get him
            yet.

                    STOSH
            You hold him. I'll slug him.

                    HOFFY
            It's not Schulz. It's that
            stoolie. Whoever he is, he's
            sure batting a thousand.

                    PRICE
            The guy I want to talk to is
            Sefton. Where's Sefton?
                    (Turns to Cookie,
                     who is coming up
                     in the line)
            You haven't seen Sefton, have you?

                    COOKIE
                    (Frightened)
            No, I haven't.

                    GERMAN GUARD
                    (Hurrying them along)
            Der Naechste!

61.   . INT. BARRACK 4 - (DAY)

The P.O.W.s are coming back with the blankets. Schulz
is standing at the door with radio and earphones.

                    SCHULZ
                    (Calling out to
                     the guards)
            Henkel! Krause!
                    (To Hoffy)
            I'm very sorry about the mouse
            trap, but the war news are very
            depressing anyway.

The two German guards have entered. Schulz points
at the rolled-up volley ball net under one of the
bunks.

                    SCHULZ
            I might as well also confiscate
            the antenna.

The guards carry out the wire-roll.

> SCHULZ
> American know-how!

Simultaneously, he snaps the wash line. Shaking with laughter, he exits. As he goes out, Cookie squeezes himself into the barrack, carrying his blanket. He starts edging towards his bunk, but Hoffy grabs him.

> HOFFY
> All right, Cookie, let's hear it: where is Sefton?

> COOKIE
> I don't know. I told you.

> PRICE
> He wouldn't be at the Kommandant's, would he?

> COOKIE
> I don't know.

> HOFFY
> What did they trade him for the radio?

> COOKIE
> I don't know.

During this, they have backed him up towards his bunk.

> HARRY
> Why don't we just look in those footlockers?

> STOSH
> Come on, you little stooge. Hand over them keys.

> COOKIE
> I haven't got any keys.

> STOSH
> Okay. Then I'll get me a key.

He grabs off a piece of iron holding up a corner of the distillery. Meanwhile, Harry has pulled out Sefton's footlockers. Stosh shoves the iron bar into one of the locks. Stops. Looks up at Hoffy.

> STOSH
> Okay, Hoffy?

> HOFFY
> Okay.

Stosh starts ripping off the lock.

Cookie has shrunk back into the corner of his bunk.

The first footlocker is cracked open. It is brimful
of cigarettes, chocolate bars, coffee, tea and sugar.
Stosh now pries open the second footlocker. He throws
back the top: there is a dazzling assortment of
cameras, binoculars, wristwatches, beer steins,
bottles of Rhine wine and a cuckoo clock.

> STOSH
> Of all the hoarding cruds!

> **BAGRADIAN**
> Looks like Macey's basement, don't
> it?

> DUNBAR
> That kid's richer than my mother.

Harry has picked up the cuckoo clock. It opens, the
birdie emerges and cuckoos.

> HARRY
> Shut up!

He slaps the door shut on it. Stosh pulls from under
the binoculars a pair of silk stockings. He holds
them up.

> STOSH
> For cryin' out loud! What would
> he be doing with these?

> DUKE'S VOICE
> Suppose you ask me.

They turn. In the door stands Duke, breathless. He
had just come in from the Compound.

> DUKE
> Go on, ask me! Because I got
> the goods on Mister Sefton. Be-
> cause this time he didn't shake me.

He moves toward the telescope at the window.

> DUKE
> Take a look for yourself. It'll
> curdle your guts.

He swings the telescope around so it faces the
Russian Compound.

> STOSH
> The Russian women!

They all dash towards the window and the telescope.
Hoffy pushes through and looks himself, focusing
the telescope.

>   DUKE
>   Try the end barrack. Where the
>   goodies are.

Hoffy looks.

>   HARRY
>   (Impatiently)
>   Come on, Hoffy! We all want to
>   see!

Hoffy straightens up. Stosh pushes Harry away and
looks through the telescope.

>   HOFFY
>   (To Duke)
>   How did he get over there?

>   DUKE
>   Easy! Walked right through the
>   gate, past the guard. Like he
>   was some Kraut Field Marshal.

Stosh, looking through the telescope, has let go
with a long whistle.

>   STOSH
>   This is murder!

62.   RUSSIAN BARRACK - (DAY)

The telescope is focused on the window, revealing:

A party is in progress. Sefton is the only man among
some eight Russian women. He lies on a bunk, reclin-
ing like a Sultan. The Russian women around him vie
for his favor. One plays the balalaika. Another is
dancing the Kazatski on the table.

63.   INT. BARRACK 4

The men struggle to get at the telescope. Harry jerks
Stosh away. Meanwhile, Blondie moves in.

>   HARRY
>   (Pulling Blondie off)
>   Go play with your marbles!

Harry looks.

                         STOSH
         The stinkin' miser! Keeping all
         that to himself!

                         TRIZ
         Would I like to lay my hands on
         him!

                         HARRY
                    (From the telescope)
         Who wants to lay their hands on
         him?

Blondie, Bagradian and a couple others have dashed to
the footlocker, grabbed themselves some binoculars,
and dash back to the window to look.

                         DUKE
                    (To Hoffy and Price)
         So I'm a vigilante, huh? So what
         are the Barrack Officers going to
         do now?

                         PRICE
         Don't worry Duke. We'll handle
         it from here on in.

                         DUKE
         You better handle it fast. Before
         a few more of us get knocked off.

Hoffy, boiling mad, grabs the telescope from the guys
and flings it across the room.

The telescope smashes against Sefton's bunk. It almost
hits Cookie. He cringes back.

DISSOLVE TO:

64.   EXT. COMPOUND - (DUSK)

         Sefton is coming back from the Russian compound. There
         are about a dozen P.O.W.s about. He pauses at the gate
         until a couple of P.O.W.s have moved on. Then he walks
         through the gate, giving the German guard a little high
         sign. Whistling a Russian tune, Sefton crosses toward
         Barrack 4.

65.   INT. BARRACK 4 - (DUSK)

         The electric lights are burning. Sefton enters,
         whistling. Duke slips behind him, slams the door
         shut, and stands there blocking the exit.

1-31-52

Sefton stops whistling. He surveys the situation.
About twenty-five P.O.W.s stand around silently,
looking at him. Hoffy, Price, Harry and Stosh in
the foreground.

> SEFTON
> (Casually)

Hi.

No answer.

> SEFTON

Too late for chow?

No answer.

> SEFTON

What's the matter, boys? Is my
slip showing?

> HOFFY

I'll say it is. You spilled a
little borscht on it.

> SEFTON

Borscht?

> STOSH

Have a nice time over there?

> SEFTON

Oh! Somebody was peeking!

He nonchalantly starts peeling off his coat.

> SEFTON

Yeah! Had a dreamy time! Those
dames, they really know how to
throw a party. I've handled
some pretty interesting material
in my day, but between you and me,
there's just nothing like the hot
breath of the Cossacks. There's
a couple of blonde snipers over
there, real man-killers...

He breaks off as his eyes fall on his footlockers.
He sees that they have been broken open.

> SEFTON

What's this?

They just look at him. He turns to Cookie, who is
curled up in his bunk, petrified.

                    SEFTON
          What happened, Cookie? Who
          did it?

                    HOFFY
          We did it.

                    SEFTON
          There better not be anything
          missing. This is private property.

                    PRICE
          So was the radio private property.
          So was Manfredi and Johnson.

                    SEFTON
          What about the radio?

                    DUKE
               (Moving in on Sefton)
          Yeah, what about it?
               (To Hoffy and Price)
          Cut the horsing around. We know
          he's the stoolie and we know what
          the pay-off is. Let's get on with
          it.

                    SEFTON
          Let's get on with what? What is
          this anyway? A Kangaroo Court?
          Why don't you get a rope and do
          it right?

                    DUKE
          You make my mouth water.

                    SEFTON
          You're all wire happy, boys.
          You've been in this camp too
          long. You put two and two to-
          gether and it comes out four.
          Only it ain't four.

                    HOFFY
          What's it add up to you, Sefton?

                    SEFTON
          It adds up that you got yourselves
          the wrong guy. Because I'm telling
          you. The Krauts wouldn't plant two
          stoolies in one barrack. And what-
          ever you do to me you're going to
          have to do all over again when you
          find the right guy.

                    BLONDIE
               (From the window)
          Watch it!

     He snaps the wash.

66.   EXT. COMPOUND - (NIGHT BY NOW)

Planks have been laid from the Administration
Building to Barrack 4. Two German guards are just
putting down the last plank right against the
barrack. Von Scherbach strides down the planks. He
is accompanied by his aide and two German soldiers.
They, of course, are marching through the mud. The
aide hurries ahead to open the door to the barrack.

67.   INT. BARRACK 4 - (NIGHT)

Von Scherbach enters, followed by his aide. All the
P.O.W.s look on tensely.

                    VON SCHERBACH
          Good evening, Sergeants.
               (Looking around)
          A bit dank in here, isn't it? ...
          Where is the Baracken-Fuehrer?

                    HOFFY
               (Stepping up)
          Yes, sir.

                    VON SCHERBACH
          You have a Lieutenant here...

He holds out his hand. His aide hands him a slip of
paper.

                    VON SCHERBACH
               (Reading)
          ... a Lieutenant James Dunbar?

                    HOFFY
          Yes, sir.

                    DUNBAR
          I am Lieutenant Dunbar.

                    VON SCHERBACH
          What is your number?

                    DUNBAR
               (Reading off his
                dog-tags)
          105-353.

                    VON SCHERBACH
               (Checking with paper)
          That is correct.
               (He salutes)

1-30-52

VON **SCHERBACH**
Lieutenant Dunbar, I came to
apologize for the accommodations.
Ordinarily, of course, we never
put officers up with enlisted
men.

DUNBAR
I'll live.

VON **SCHERBACH**
Quite a transportation jam we
are having outside of Frankfurt!
They are very angry in Berlin.
They will be even angrier on the
East Front, waiting for that
ammunition train. Don't you think
so, Lieutenant?

DUNBAR
I don't know what you're talking
about, Colonel.

VON **SCHERBACH**
Of course you don't. Now, Lieutenant,
how would you like to join me in
my quarters? I have a nice fire
going.

DUNBAR
I'm okay here. Why bother?

VON **SCHERBACH**
No bother. I'm very grateful
for a little company. You see,
I suffer from insomnia.

DUNBAR
Ever try forty sleeping pills?

VON **SCHERBACH**
(To his aide, sharply)
Abfuehren!

The aide takes Dunbar by the arm.

HOFFY
(To the aide)
Wait a minute. We have some
rights here.
(To von **Scherbach**)
Why is this man being taken
out?

                    VON SCHERBACH
              (Looking around the room)
          Curtains would do wonders for
          this barrack.
              (On second thought)
          You will not get them.

He snaps his fingers. The aide marches Dunbar out.
Von Scherbach follows, slamming the door after him.

For a moment, there is a stunned silence.   Then:

                    BAGRADIAN
          How did he ever find out about
          that ammunition train?

                    HOFFY
          You must have shot off your
          mouth all the way from
          Frankfurt to here.

                    BAGRADIAN
          . We did not.

                    PRICE
          Maybe just a hint or so. Think
          hard.

                    BAGRADIAN
          I don't have to think. We didn't
          tell anything to anybody. Not a
          word. Not until we hit this
          barrack.

The men stand struck.

Then all eyes go to Sefton. He is closing his footlockers. He senses their look. Straightens up.

                    SEFTON
          What are you looking at me for?

No answer. He shoves the footlockers under his bunk.
From OFF come whistles and shouts: 'Lights Out!'

The lights go out. The barrack is in semi-darkness.

                    SEFTON
          I suppose some jerk's going to
          say I did it.

1-30-52

He crawls into his bunk. He lies there, his eyes
wide open. The air is charged.

After a long moment, the men move in on him, led by
Duke and Stosh. Sefton sits up to meet them. A
couple of guys grab him from behind, hold him down.

>   SEFTON
>   Why don't you try it one at a
>   time?

The first blows are falling.

Joey lies in his bunk, his head propped against the
bedpost, his face still in idiotic Hitler make-up.
He does not comprehend the SOUNDS from Sefton's
bunk, the beating and muffled cries. In the foreground, the electric bulb, hanging straight, sways
gently.

FADE OUT

                    END OF SEQUENCE D

<u>SEQUENCE E</u>

FADE IN:

68.		<u>EXT. COMPOUND</u>							COOKIE'S VOICE

Wintry day. Cold sun					Now, there's a lot of folks
shining. Through the big				around these days that don't
gate two vehicles are					believe in Santa Claus. I
driving into the compound:				always did and I always
a 1939 Buick sedan and a				will. For a while there,
tarpaulin-covered truck.				I thought the German Luft-
The vehicles are muddy,					waffe had shot him down,
battered, and carry the					reindeer, sleigh and all.
insignia of the Red Cross.				But, no sir! Come the day
They stop in front of the				before Christmas, he showed
Administration Building.				up with some presents for
P.O.W.s converge from all				us, the Geneva Man did. He
sides. Out of the Buick				had started out with seven
steps the Geneva Man: a					truckloads. He was lucky
friendly type, about fifty-				to get one of them through -
five, dressed in civilian				with all the bombing and
clothes and carrying a					booby traps and pilfering.
brief case. He tips his				Still, they were presents
Homburg to the P.O.W.s, but				and made you feel good:
they are more interested in				coffee, a little sugar and
the truck. While a couple				some candy and toothbrushes
of German lieutenants ex-				and about a thousand rolls
change credentials with the				of that sanitary paper.
Geneva Man, the Red Cross				Brother, they sure kept
drivers roll back the tar-				sending us reams of that
paulin of the truck, and				stuff. I'll bet you
the P.O.W.s (including all				if they had dropped all
the men from Barrack 4, ex-				that paper on Berlin the
cept Sefton) crowd around				first day, the war would
the goodies.							have been over right then
										and there.

69.		<u>INT. BARRACK 4 - (DAY)</u>

It is quite changed now. The wash is gone. Everything
is put away. The barrack is apparently empty, except
for a German guard and Schulz, who gives the place a
last once-over. The German guard is sweeping dust
under the bunks.

						SCHULZ
				Schnell! Schnell! Bevor der
				Mann vom Roten Kreuz inspizieren
				kommt!

At one of the bunks he sees a miserable plant, potted
in a smelly old shoe. He picks it up and gives it to
the guard.

                              SCHULZ
                    Nehmen Sie das hinaus!

The guard takes the shoe out. Schulz, about to leave
himself, sees a pair of socks hanging from the line
above. He rips them down and tucks them disgustedly
under a blanket. From OFF comes:

                         SEFTON'S VOICE
                    Hey, Schulz!

Schulz turns.

At the other end of the barrack, Sefton is lying in
his bunk. He has propped himself up on his elbow.
His face is battered. One eye is swollen, one ear
gashed. His body is aching.

                              SCHULZ
                         (Crossing)
                    What is this? You must get out
                    of the bunk. The Geneva Man is
                    coming to inspect the barrack!

He sees Sefton's condition.

                              SCHULZ
                    Du lieber Gott! How do you
                    look? You had a fight?

                              SEFTON
                         (Holding out a
                          pair of silk
                          stockings)
                    How would you like to give Frau
                    Schulz a pair of silk stockings
                    for Christmas?

                              SCHULZ
                    You should go and see the doctor.
                    Maybe I can --
                         (Breaking off)
                    Silk stockings?

                              SEFTON
                    Here. Take them.

He presses the stockings upon Schulz.

                              SCHULZ
                    Wunderbar! Maybe they are too
                    wunderbar for my wife. But
                    there is a piano teacher in
                    the village --

90

                            SEFTON
             And how about three hundred
             cigarettes for yourself?

He has dragged himself out of his bunk and is taking
cartons of cigarettes out of the footlocker.

                            SCHULZ
             Three hundred cigarettes! What
             is it you want from me?

                            SEFTON
             Who's the guy, Schulz?

                            SCHULZ
             What guy?

                            SEFTON
             The one you work with. Who is he?
             How do you do it?

                            SCHULZ
             I do not want those cigarettes.

                            SEFTON
              Yes, you do!

He pulls himself up with an armful of cartons.

                            SEFTON
              I'll make it five hundred!

                            SCHULZ
             No! No!

Sefton grabs him.

                            SEFTON
             You'd better talk, Schulz, because
             I'm going to find out with you or
             without you. Because I won't let
             go for a second. Because they'll
             have to kill me to stop me. So talk!

                            SCHULZ
             Talk what? I do not know
             anything!

                            SEFTON
             How many do you want? A thousand?

He bends over the footlocker, fighting his pain,
comes up with more cartons. He thrusts them upon
Schulz.

                          91

                              SEFTON
                Take it!   Take it!

There is a SOUND of P.O.W.s entering. Schulz looks
off.

The P.O.W.s are coming back from the compound with
the Christmas presents. Hoffy, Price, Duke, Harry and
Stosh stand in the door, looking at Sefton and Schulz.

Schulz quickly drops the cartons on Sefton's bunk.
Stands embarrassed for a moment, then retrieves his
poise.

                              SCHULZ
                Gentlemen! When the Geneva Man
                comes through the barrack, I don't
                want any funny business. No
                mustaches. We will all behave ourselves.

He goes toward the other end of the barrack, which
is by now filled with all the other P.O.W.s. Schulz
stops.

                              SCHULZ
                And gentlemen!   You will not
                complain to the Geneva Man. Because
                I have orders from the Kommandant
                to report everyone who complains.

The men move toward Sefton.

                              STOSH
                Look at him! Dunbar's being
                crucified and he's trading again!

                              DUKE
                Didn't you get enough last night?
                You itching for more?

                              HARRY
                Some guys never learn!

                              HOFFY
                I called a meeting of the barrack
                chiefs this morning, Sefton. I
                thought maybe I could get you
                transferred into another barrack.
                It turns out nobody likes you any
                more than we do.

                              SEFTON
                So you're stuck with me, eh?

2-1-52

92

                         STOSH
          Maybe those Russian dames would
          take him.

                         HARRY
          Not with that kisser - not any
          more!

Cookie has come through the door with some ice in a
towel.

                         COOKIE
                    (To Sefton)
          Here ... put some ice on it.

Duke grabs the ice-bag from him.

                         DUKE
          Beat it, stooge!
                    (To Hoffy and Price)
          Go on - tell the crumb where he
          stands.

                         PRICE
          All right, Sefton. You got
          away lucky last night. One
          more move, no matter how small,
          and you'll wake up with your
          throat slit!

                         HOFFY
          You heard that, Sefton?

                         SEFTON
          Sure I heard it. I still got
          one good ear.

From OFF comes Schulz' WHISTLE. They look.

Schulz stands at the far door, blowing his whistle.

                         SCHULZ
          Achtung! Achtung! Everybody
          at attention for the Geneva
          Man!

The men all come to attention before their bunks. The
German lieutenant enters, ushering in the Geneva Man.
Schulz stiffens and clicks his heels.

                         GENEVA MAN
          As you were, gentlemen. Please.

He takes off his hat, looks around, and as the scene
progresses, moves through the barrack.

                    GERMAN LIEUTENANT
        Here we have a typical barrack.
        It houses seventy-five men.
        Every one of them has his own
        bunk, naturally.

                    GENEVA MAN
        Naturally. It would be rather
        awkward to have three men in
        one bunk.

                    GERMAN LIEUTENANT
        As for the blankets, you will
        notice they are very warm.
        Fifty percent wool.

                    GENEVA MAN
        They also smell of moth balls.
                (To a P.O.W. at that
                particular bunk)
        When were they issued? This
        morning?

        The P.O.W. looks noncommittally.

                    GENEVA MAN
                (To the Lieutenant)
        What do you do for heat in
        this barrack? No stove?

                    GERMAN LIEUTENANT
        The men here used it for a trap
        door, so we had to remove it
        temporarily.

                    GENEVA MAN
        How long is temporarily? I
        trust not until July.

        Through the other door a couple of P.O.W.s have brought
        in the chow-tub, steaming with some brew. They put it
        on the table in the middle of the barrack.

                    GERMAN LIEUTENANT
        Here you see a typical meal the
        prisoners are getting. What are
        we having today, Schulz?

                    SCHULZ
        Bean soup with ham hocks. Would
        you like to taste it?
                (Fishing with the ladle)
        Where's the ham hock? There
        should be a ham hock.

                         STOSH
               When he finds it, we'll send it
               to Geneva.

The Geneva Man continues down the barrack.

                         GENEVA MAN
               Are there any complaints? Please
               speak up.

He looks around. A pause.

                         GENEVA MAN
               Don't be afraid to talk. That's
               what the Geneva Convention is
               for: to protect the rights of
               prisoners of war. Whether they
               are Americans or Germans.

Nobody answers.

                         GENEVA MAN
                      (To Harry)
               What have you got to say?

                         HARRY
               I like it here.
                      (Then with a shrug)
               Aeh!

                         GENEVA MAN
                      (To Price)
               What about you?

                         PRICE
               It's all right. Considering.

The Geneva Man walks on. Stops at Sefton's bunk.
Sees his battered face.

                         GENEVA MAN
               What happened to you? Were you
               beaten? Why don't you answer?
                      (To the German
                      Lieutenant)
               What did you do to this man?

                         SEFTON
               They didn't do nothing.

                         GENEVA MAN
               Who beat you?

                         SEFTON
               Nobody beat me. We were playing
               pinochle. It's a rough game.

                    HOFFY
                 (Stepping up)
        Pardon me, sir. Since you want
        us to speak up, there was a man
        removed from this barrack last
        night. A Lieutenant Dunbar.
        We sure would appreciate your
        looking into it. That's if they
        haven't shot him yet.

                  GENEVA MAN
            (To the German Lieutenant)
        Why was the man arrested?

                GERMAN LIEUTENANT
        Sabotage. He blew up a train.

                    HOFFY
        They'd have to prove that first,
        wouldn't they? Isn't that what the
        Geneva Convention says? You can't
        just take a man out and shoot him!

QUICK DISSOLVE TO:

70.   INT. VON SCHERBACH'S OFFICE - (DAY)

The office is in the Administration Building. It is
primitive, sparsely furnished. A desk with a couple of
phones on it. Iron stove. A black leather sofa. Maps.

In the room are von Scherbach, Dunbar and the Colonel's
ORDERLY. The Colonel's boots, shining gloriously, stand
near the desk. He is pacing up and down in his stocking feet talking to Dunbar. In his hand is the black
queen from the chess game. He tosses it into the air
once in a while and catches it. Dunbar stands close to
a wall. He is completely exhausted, fighting sleep.

START the SCENE on the chess piece in von Scherbach's
hand and PAN with it as von Scherbach walks to reveal
the room.

                  VON SCHERBACH
        You have no idea how boring my life
        here is. If it weren't for an
        occasional air raid or some foolish
        prisoners trying to escape, I
        wouldn't know what to do. I want
        to thank you for keeping me company.
        I don't drink, I don't smoke, I don't
        read. I hate music. That only
        leaves good conversation. It will
        be a shame to lose you.

                        DUNBAR
                     (Fighting sleep)
          I didn't do it -- I didn't
          do it.

                        VON SCHERBACH
          Of course you did! Twenty-six
          carloads of munitions gone off
          like a trick cigar! The S.S.
          is running around in circles.
          The Gestapo is arresting the
          wrong people. And von Scherbach
          has caught the fish. Most amus-
          ing, isn't it?

Dunbar falls back against the wall, yawning.

                        VON SCHERBACH
                     (Straightening him
                      up)
          You are being rude again.

                        DUNBAR
          I want to sleep. Give me five
          minutes on that couch.

                        VON SCHERBACH
                     (Looking at his
                      wristwatch)
          Nine-thirty. General von
          Pfeffinger should be at his
          desk by now. Shall we call
          Berlin and tell him the good
          news?

                        DUNBAR
                     (Wearily)
          I didn't do it. I didn't do
          it.

Von Scherbach has gone to the desk, picks up the
phone and cranks it.

                        VON SCHERBACH
                     (Into phone)
          Hauptkommando Berlin. Gen-
          eral von Pfeffinger. Dringend.

He hangs up, sits on the edge of the desk holding
up his stocking feet. During his subsequent spiel,
the orderly steps up and pulls von Scherbach's boots
on.

> VON SCHERBACH
> I hope you appreciate this moment,
> Lieutenant. You see, I am a cavalry
> man. All the von Scherbachs were
> cavalry men. Well, you know what
> happened to the cavalry. The young
> ones they put into panzer divisions.
> The older ones they put in the
> quartermaster's corps. Or they
> made them recruiting officers or
> wardens. Like me. Wet nurses to
> putrid prisoners. In Berlin they
> have forgotten that Colonel von
> Scherbach even exists. They will
> remember now!

The boots are on. The telephone RINGS. He jumps to
his feet, picks up the receiver, automatically clicks
his heels.

> VON SCHERBACH
> (Into phone)
> Berlin? Hier Oberst von Scherbach.
> General von Pfeffinger?
> (Clicks his heels)
> Oberst von Scherbach. Stalag 17.
> Melde gehorchsamst haben als
> Gefangenen den Mann, der Munitionszug
> in Frankfurt in die Luft gesprengt
> hat. Jawohl, Herr General -
> (Clicks the heels)
> - Name Leutenant Dunbar. Sabotage.
> Jawohl, Herr General.

He clicks his heels again, hangs up. Sits again on
the desk and the orderly automatically starts to pull
off his boots.

> VON SCHERBACH
> There will be two S.S. men here
> tomorrow to take you to Berlin.
> You will be interrogated by the
> General Staff. When you come to
> the part about your arrest, I'm
> sure you won't forget to give
> me the proper credit.

> DUNBAR
> (Sinking back)
> I want to sleep ... I haven't
> slept for three days.

                    VON SCHERBACH
                  (Pulling him up)
          You will remember the name? Von
          Scherbach? VON SCHER-BACH!

There's a KNOCK on the door.

                    VON SCHERBACH
              Herein!

Schulz opens the door, clicks his heels, salutes.

                    SCHULZ
          Der Mann vom Roten Kreuz moechte
          den Herrn Oberst sprechen!

                    VON SCHERBACH
              Ich bitte!

Schulz ushers in the Geneva Man, steps out himself.

                    VON SCHERBACH
          Well, Herr Inspector! How did
          you find the camp? Crowded but
          gemuetlich, shall we say?

                    GENEVA MAN
          I want to talk about Lieutenant
          Dunbar. Is this Lieutenant
          Dunbar?

                    VON SCHERBACH
              It is.

                    GENEVA MAN
          What exactly is he charged
          with?

                    VON SCHERBACH
          Whatever it is, it's out of your
          jurisdiction. This man is not a
          prisoner of war. Not any more.
          He is a saboteur.

                    GENEVA MAN
          He is a prisoner of war until you
          can prove sabotage.

                    DUNBAR
          I didn't do it. I was in the
          Frankfurt station and the train
          was three miles away when it
          blew up.

VON SCHERBACH
Oh, come now! You threw a time
bomb.

DUNBAR
How could I have had a time
bomb? They searched me when
they took me prisoner.

GENEVA MAN
And the way you search your
prisoners, it does sound rather
unlikely.

VON SCHERBACH
All I know is he did it. I am
satisfied.

GENEVA MAN
I am not. According to the
Geneva Convention --

DUNBAR
Is there anything about letting
a guy sleep in the Geneva Convention?

He has shuffled over to the sofa, and plunks himself
down - instantly asleep.

VON SCHERBACH
(To the Geneva Man)
You were saying - ?

GENEVA MAN
Simply this. After the hostilities
are ended, there will be such a
thing as a War Crimes Commission.
If this man should be convicted
without proper proof, you will be
held responsible, Colonel von
Scherbach.

VON SCHERBACH
Interesting.

GENEVA MAN
Isn't it?

The Geneva Man looks straight into von Scherbach's
eyes. Von Scherbach doesn't like the look. He picks
up the black queen and tosses it again.

                              VON SCHERBACH
                    Very well. If you insist on
                    details. I have ways of finding
                    out about that blasted time
                    bomb. Good day, sir.
                         (Indicating
                          stocking feet)
                    You will forgive me for receiving
                    you like this?

                              GENEVA MAN
                    Perfectly all right. I do not
                    like boots.

          As the Geneva Man exits -

                              VON SCHERBACH
                    Schulz!

          Schulz enters.

                              VON SCHERBACH
                    Wie ist es moeglich dass dieser
                    Amerikaner eine Bombe bei sich
                    hatte? Er wurde doch bei der
                    Gefangennahme untersucht.

                              SCHULZ
                    Jawohl, Herr Kommandant.

                              VON SCHERBACH
                    Finden Sie es heraus - und zwar
                    sofort!

                              SCHULZ
                    Zu Befehl, Herr Kommandant.

          Von Scherbach tosses him the black queen.

          QUICK DISSOLVE TO:

71.   INT. BARRACK 4 - (DAY)

          START ON black queen now with the other chess pieces
          on the table. PAN UP to disclose the barrack and
          the electric light, its cord now looped.

          Sefton is lying in his bunk, dressed. Cookie above
          him in his bunk. At the center table, Harry, Stosh,
          Blondie and Bagradian are decorating the Christmas
          tree with their dogtags and hand-made candles. Joey
          sits there watching them. Blondie takes off Joey's
          dogtags and puts them on the tree. One of the
          P.O.W.s is WHISTLING Silent Night.

          2-1-52

Sitting on a stool is Triz. He is knitting a little
baby's garment. He pauses as a thought disturbs him,
then:

                    TRIZ
          I believe it. I believe it.

He goes on with the knitting.

Through the door come Duke and Price, followed by
two P.O.W.s from another barrack. One P.O.W. is
carrying an old-fashioned phonograph, the other
some records.

                    DUKE
               (Indicating
                  center table)
          Put it down, boys.

                    HARRY
          Hey, - music!

                    PRICE
          We made a deal with Barrack One.

                    BAGRADIAN
               (To Price)
          Any news on Dunbar?

                    PRICE
          He's still in the Kommandant's
          office. That's all I know.

The P.O.W.s from Barrack One have deposited the
phonograph and the records on the table.

                    DUKE
          Over here.

They follow him to Sefton's bunk.

                    DUKE
               (To Cookie)
          Let's have that distillery.   Come
          on.

Cookie looks down at Sefton for permission.

                    DUKE
          What are you looking at him for?
               (To Sefton)
          Any objections, Sefton?

                    SEFTON
          Take it.

2-1-52

The P.O.W.s climb on Sefton's bunk and start taking
down the distillery, which is piled up in Cookie's
bunk.

>   DUKE
>   (To Sefton)
>   Next we're going to auction off
>   your department store -- and
>   your stable.

>   SEFTON
>   Why not?

At the table, Price finishes cranking the machine.
Harry puts on a record and Price starts it playing.
The tune is: When Johnny Comes Marching Home. The
guys start crowding around.

Meanwhile, Stosh has been watching the P.O.W.s from
Barrack One take down the distillery. As they start
out, he grabs up an empty glass jar, follows them
surreptitiously and, in moving, siphons off a stream
of booze into the glass jar. One of the P.O.W.s
catches him.

>   P.O.W.
>   (Slapping his hand)
>   Hey! That goes with it!

They pull the hose out of the glass jar and leave.
Stosh, however, has gotten himself a pint of Schnapps.

At the table Harry and a few others start singing with
the record. Everybody has gathered around except Sefton
and Cookie. Price moves over to his bunk, (PAN with
him). As he takes off his jacket his eyes fall on -

The loop in the electric cord.

Price. His eyes narrow for a split second. Then he
takes his cap off, cases the situation. The P.O.W.s
are at the phonograph. Sefton lies in his bunk, his
eyes toward the wall. Cookie climbs down to join the
others. Nonchalantly, Price crosses toward the lamp.
He stands at the table with his back towards the barrack. Picks up the black queen, pulls the top off,
palms a small piece of paper, puts the top back and
places the chess piece back on the chess board. He
is about to read, but -

Some of the P.O.W.s come marching down the barrack
toward Price in a take-off of a homecoming parade,
led by Harry and Stosh.

Price stands there, the note in his fist. After they
have passed, he opens his hand, reads the palmed note,
puts it in his pocket. He looks after the others who
are now marching down at the other end of the barrack.
Casually, he pulls the slip noose out of the light
cord, and walks toward the center table.

Sefton, lying in his bunk, sees the shadow of the bulb
and the light cord on the wall, swinging gently back
and forth. It doesn't make too much of an impression
on him. However, he definitely notices it and looks
around for the cause. He dismisses it and lies back
in his bunk.

The Johnny Comes Marching Home number is over and
Bagradian now goes into an impersonation of Lionel
Barrymore, as the mayor of a small town, welcoming home
the returning warriors -- and Jimmy Stewart answering
for the soldiers. (To be worked out later). During
this, Price has joined them.

                    P.O.W.s
          Do Bogart.
          Do Cary Grant.

                    PRICE
          Do Cagney.

                    STOSH
          Naw! Do Grable!

                    BAGRADIAN
          Okay.

He goes into a short impersonation of Clark Gable.

                    STOSH
          Grable, not Gable!

                    HARRY
          Do Jimmy Durante!

                    PRICE
          Do Cagney. Like you did yesterday.

                    BAGRADIAN
               (A la Cagney)
          There was that ammunition train in
          the depot at Frankfurt, see? So
          Dunbar gets himself in the men's
          room and fixes a time bomb, see?
          Then he waits until the train
          starts moving out, see? And one
          of the cars got the door open with
          some straw on the floor, see? So
          he throws it, see, and three minutes
          later - voom! See?

                    PRICE
Throws what? How could he have
a time bomb?

                    BAGRADIAN
Just pulled the old match gag,
see!

                    PRICE
What's the match gag?

                    BAGRADIAN
Take some matches, see?
        (Takes a book of matches
        from his pocket)
And a cigarette, see?
        (Takes a burning
        cigarette from
        Triz' mouth)
Tuck the cigarette in like this,
see?
        (Tucks the cigarette
        inside cover of match-
        book with the lit end
        sticking out)
Now the cigarette keeps burning
like a fuse, see?

                    DUKE
Say, that's a dandy!

                    PRICE
        (As it sinks in)
Yeah. Pretty clever.

                    STOSH
Do Grable.

                    HARRY
Hey, here's Esther Williams.

He bends his head over and taps his ear, as if to
shake out water. No laugh.

                    HARRY
Nothing, eh?

                    P.O.W.
Do Cary Grant.

Bagradian goes into a take-off on Cary Grant. Price
leans his head against a bunk-post, completely relaxed.

DISSOLVE TO:

72.   INT. BARRACK 4 - (EVENING)

The lights are on. In the foreground, our bulb, with
a loop in the cord again. A Christmas party is in
progress. On the center table, the pitiful little
tree is lit. All the P.O.W.s in the barrack are huddled around the table, most of them sitting on the
bunks. They are singing Adeste Fideles. It is bitter
cold. Outside the wind is howling. They are wrapped
in blankets and most of them wear gloves.

As for Sefton, he is lying in his bunk, a pariah.
Duke comes over from the group, pulls Sefton's footlocker out and starts taking out the bottles of Rhine
wine.

                    DUKE
            Where's the corkscrew?

He finds it, puts it in his pocket.

                    SEFTON
            Have a cigar.

                    DUKE
            Thanks.

He takes a cigar, puts it in his mouth and goes off
with the wine. As Sefton looks after him, his eyes
are caught by the light cord and the noose in it. He
stares at it.

The P.O.W.s around the tree are SINGING, Price
prominently in the foreground. Duke has come with
the wine and starts opening it. Stosh nudges Joey
who sits next to him and points to a lone little
package under the tree.

                    STOSH
            Hey, Joey - there's a present
            for you.

Joey doesn't move. Stosh picks it up.

                    STOSH
            Want me to open it for you?

He opens it. It's the crude ocarina he carved out
of wood. Joey's eyes flicker. He takes the ocarina
and starts playing weird SOUNDS on it. The boys
look at him, delighted.

                    STOSH
            There, Joey - ain't that better
            than being a lawyer?

                    HARRY
                 (Nudging Stosh)
        Animal! Got a little something
        for you!

He produces from behind his back a package, wrapped
with ersatz ribbon.

                    STOSH
        Got a little something for you,
        too!

He takes out a package from inside his blanket.

                    HARRY
        I'll open mine now.

                    STOSH
        I'll open mine, too.

They start opening their presents. It becomes apparent
that each has given the other a roll of sanitary paper.

                 HARRY AND STOSH
              (Throwing their arms
                 around each other)
        You're a doll!
        Just what I wanted!
        How did you know!

From the compound, a SIREN is heard. And shouts,
Lights Out! The singing stops.

                    PRICE
        Air raid warning.

                    BLONDIE
        Not Christmas Eve!

                    HOFFY
                 (Wearily)
        Come on, everybody. Let's get
        out. Let's hit those slit
        trenches.

                    TRIZ
                 (Getting up)
        I'm not really built for war.

They blow out the candles. Simultaneously, the lights
are turned off. The men start rushing out. Outside,
through the door, men from other barracks can be seen
hurrying by.

Sefton sits up in his bunk, looking at the electric
cord. The bulb is dark now.

                  SCHULZ' VOICE
         Out, out everybody!

Sefton looks off.

Schulz has come through the door and is herding them
out.

                  SCHULZ
         You must get out. For your own
         good, you must get out.

                  HOFFY
         Come on, everybody!
            (Pushing Joey)
         Let's go!

Schulz has come up to Sefton.

                  SCHULZ
         What's the matter with you?
         You want to be killed?

                  SEFTON
        Not particularly.

He picks up his leather jacket and moves toward the
door where the other P.O.W.s are crowding out.

                  PRICE
         (To Stosh and Harry
         who are lingering
         behind)
        Must you always be the last?

                  STOSH
        Oh, yeah? You jump in those
        trenches first and everybody
        jumps on top of you!

                  HARRY
        How do you think I got my
        hernia?

Price pushes them out. Dawdles at the door, closes
it from inside. He is alone with Schulz in the dark
barrack.

Schulz has gone over to the chess board, has picked
up the black queen, opened it. There is no message.
Price comes up to him.

                                   SCHULZ
                        Nun? Was ist? Haben Sie's
                        herausgefunden?

                                   PRICE
                        Ich weiss alles.

                                   SCHULZ
                        Wie hat er's gemacht?

                                   PRICE
                        Ganz einfach... Streichhoelzer...
                        und eine Zigarette...

He takes a book of matches and puts a lighted cigarette
in it.

                                   PRICE
                        Passen Sie auf!

The "time bomb" goes off, lighting up their faces.

                                   SCHULZ
                        Ach so! ... ACH SO!

There is a broad grin on his face. Then he and Price
move out of the barrack, quickly. As they go out the
door -

                                   SCHULZ
                              (Calling off, with
                               phony efficiency)
                        Air raid! Air raid! Everybody
                        in the trenches!

Now the barrack is empty. Except for one thing: from
behind one of the rear bunks, Sefton steps out. He
puts a cigar in his mouth, lights it. There is a
gleam in his eye.

                                   SEFTON
                        Ach so-o-o-o!

FADE OUT

                        END OF SEQUENCE E

SEQUENCE F

FADE IN:

73.   INT. BARRACKS 4 - (DAY)

	COOKIE'S VOICE

The phonograph, on the center table, is playing: I Love You. About a dozen P.O.W.s are dancing with each other, among them, Triz, leading Harry, Blondie, leading a bearded P.O.W. The whole thing is very elegant, with new guys cutting in, politely. One of the P.O.W.s sings into a mike, consisting of a stick stuck into a knothole in the table with a tin can on top.

COOKIE'S VOICE
So it got to be Christmas Day in Stalag 17. As it turned out, it was more like the Fourth of July -- with all the fireworks that were to go off all at once and bust the camp wide open. It sure started off innocently enough, with a party going on in every barracks...

Sefton, propped up in his bunk, is watching the proceedings. In back of him, against the window, sits Cookie. Sefton's eyes never leave -

Price, who is near the phonograph with Pirelli and another P.O.W. They are supplying a makeshift jazz accompaniment, playing on a washboard, drumming on the table and strumming a bass fiddle string attached to a bucket.

Sefton. There is a look of cynical amusement on his face as he takes this in.

A P.O.W. tags Triz to cut in. Harry holds out his arms. He is ready. But the P.O.W. dances off with Triz, leaving Harry flat. Harry looks over to Stosh.

Stosh lies in his bunk, drinking what's left of the booze he swiped from the distillery. He is staring at the pin-ups of Grable pasted on the ceiling of his bunk.

                    HARRY
          Come on, Animal - let's trip the
          light fantastic!

                    STOSH
          Let me alone.

                    HARRY
          You're crying, Animal.

                    STOSH
          It's that song, Harry!

                    HARRY
               (Seeing the pin-up)
          You don't want to cry over a
          dame that doesn't even know
          you're alive! Snap out of it!

                    STOSH
          There's a time in every man's
          life when he wants to be alone!
          So go away!

He takes another swig and lets down the big pin-up
so it hangs a few inches in front of his eyes.

Harry turns away from Stosh, picks up a pilot cap,
turns it inside out so the yellow fur shows on top,
puts it on. He gets some straw out of a hole in a
mattress and tucks it under the cap like curls.

                    HARRY
          All right, boys, Who wants the
          Queen of the May?

A P.O.W. drops his partner and dances Harry off.

Sefton, in his bunk, watching Price all the time.

                    SEFTON
          Any cigars left, Cookie?

No answer from Cookie.

                    SEFTON
          Come on, Cookie. Get me a
          cigar.

Cookie doesn't move.

                    SEFTON
          What's the matter? You on their
          team now? You think I'm the guy?

                    COOKIE
          I don't know anymore.

Sefton goes to the raided footlocker for a last
tattered cigar.

                    SEFTON
          I understand how you feel, Cookie.
          It's sort of rough -- one American
          squealing on other Americans.
               (Lights his cigar)

111

SEFTON

Then again, Cookie -- maybe that
stoolie's not an American at all.
Maybe he's a German the Krauts
planted in this barracks. They do
this type of thing. Just put an
agent in with us - a trained
specialist. Lots of loose information floating around a prison camp.
Not just whether somebody wants to
escape, but what outfits we were
with and where we were stationed,
and how our radar operates. Could
be, couldn't it?

COOKIE

In this barracks?

SEFTON

Why not? Just one of the boys.
Sharing our bunks. Eating our
chow. Right in amongst the ones
that beat me up. Except that he
beat hardest.

COOKIE

Who is it?

SEFTON

That's not the point, Cookie. The
point is what do you do with him?
You tip your mitt and the Jerries
pull him out of here and plant him
someplace else, like Stalag Sixteen
or Fifteen. Or you kill him off
and the Krauts turn around and kill
off the whole barracks. Every one
of us. So what do you do?

COOKIE

Who is it?

Sefton doesn't answer.

COOKIE

If you don't want to tell me,
why don't you tell Hoffy? Or
Security?

SEFTON

Yeah. Security.

ro   105.

He just sits there, smoking and looking in the
direction of -

Price at the middle table. Bagradian steps up to
Price, who is busy beating out the rhythm. The P.O.W.
is no longer singing.

                    BAGRADIAN
          Where's Hoffy? Why don't we get
          any news about Dunbar?

                    PRICE
          Don't worry. He'll be all right.

                    BAGRADIAN
          I had to be the ham! I had to
          shoot off my mouth!

                    PRICE
          Forget it. He'll be back here.
          They've got no proof.

Harry seats himself on the table, tossing his curls.

                    HARRY
               (To the rhythm boys)
          Sweet and soft, boys. Beguile
          me.

Stosh in his bunk. He drains the booze from the jar,
looks out at the room through tear blurred eyes. He
sees:

Harry sitting on the table, listening to the music.
He is in the identical pose Betty Grable has struck
in the big pin-up photo.

Stosh's eyes go back to the big pin-up photo. He
looks back at:

Harry. By now it is not Harry who is sitting there.
It is Betty Grable, or rather the pin-up photo superimposed in the same size as Harry.

Stosh blinks his eyes. He stares some more. Delirious
happiness dawns on his face. He climbs out of his
bunk and walks toward Harry, in a trance.

                    STOSH
               (To himself)
          Betty! ... Betty!

He has reached the table, bows politely to Harry.

                    STOSH
          May I have this dance, Miss?

>   HARRY
>   Why, sure!

He climbs off the table. Stosh puts his arm around
very elegantly and dances him off.

>   STOSH
>   Who would've ever thought I'd
>   be holding you in my arms?

A peculiar expression comes over Harry's face.

>   STOSH
>   Pinch me, will you? Pinch me
>   so I'll know I'm not dreaming.

Harry reaches up and pinches him heartily on the
cheek.

>   STOSH
>   Thank you, darling!

Again, a reaction from Harry as they dance on. Stosh
sings a few bars of I Love You with the record. His
cheek is very close to Harry. He is lost in blissful
romance.

>   STOSH
>   Did anybody ever tell you you have
>   the most beautiful legs in the
>   world?

Harry does a big take.

>   STOSH
>   But it's not just those legs.
>   It's that nose of yours I'm
>   crazy about. That cute little
>   button of a nose!

>   HARRY
>   (The situation begins
>   to seep through)
>   Hey, Animal! Animal!

>   STOSH
>   (Sweeping on madly)
>   I've been crazy about you for
>   years. I've seen every picture
>   you've ever made six times. I'd
>   just sit there and never even
>   open that popcorn bag.

>   HARRY
>   (Breaking from him)
>   Animal! Animal! Wake up!

He starts slapping his face.

> STOSH
> Betty! Betty!

> HARRY
> (Taking off his wig)
> This is me, Animal! It's Harry
> Shapiro!

Stosh stares at him. The truth dawns on him. He
starts bawling like a child.

Hoffy hurries in from the compound. He is followed
by Duke, Marko and The Crutch.

> HOFFY
> Cut that music! Cut it! Listen!

All turn.

> HOFFY
> The S. S. Men are here to pick up
> Dunbar. They're taking him to
> Berlin. Looks like he's finished.

> DUKE
> Only he ain't quite finished yet.
> Blondie - get that smudge pot.
> Tie it to Steve's leg.

Blondie gets the can of smoke-powder and, as the scene
progresses, fastens it in The Crutch's empty pants'
leg.

> PRICE
> What are you going to do?

> HOFFY
> I want everybody out of here.
> We'll need a lot of commotion
> on the compound.

> MARKO
> I'll get the men from the other
> barracks.

> PRICE
> (To Hoffy)
> You don't think you can snatch
> Dunbar? Not from the S.S.?

> HOFFY
> We're sure going to make a stab
> at it. You, Price and Stosh and

HOFFY (Cont'd)
Harry and Blondie - be at the
north latrine. You'll all get
your posts. Now everybody start
drifting out with Marko.

MARKO
Easy, boys, easy. Disperse out
there nicely and always remember
just because the Krauts are dumb
that doesn't make them stupid.

The men start filing out through both doors quietly.

HOFFY
(To Blondie)
Ready?

BLONDIE
Roger.

HOFFY
(To Price, Stosh, Harry
and Duke)
Okay. Move on.

The Crutch, Blondie, Harry and Stosh leave.

PRICE
I don't know what your scheme
is, but it sounds crazy.

HOFFY
Maybe it's crazy, but it's better
than having Dunbar dead.

PRICE
Just as you say, Hoffy. But
wouldn't it be smarter if I went
out and kept Schulz tied up?

HOFFY
Good.

SEFTON
(Moving in)
I wouldn't worry about Schulz.
I'd worry about Sefton. Remember
me? I'm the stoolie.

DUKE
You ain't going to squeal this
one, brother.

                    SEFTON
No? Aren't you a little afraid
to turn the stoolie loose on
that compound? For a tip-off like
this, you know what the Krauts
would pay?

                    HOFFY
You'll stay in this barracks and
not a peep out of you.

                    SEFTON
Okay, then. Put a guard on me.
I want you to put a guard on me.
Because if anything goes wrong
out there, this time you won't
have a patsy. Right?

                    HOFFY
Right.

                    SEFTON
So who stays with me? Maybe Joey?
No - not Joey. Wouldn't you feel
safer with Security on the job?

                    HOFFY
Okay, Price. You stay.

                    PRICE
What about Schulz?

                    HOFFY
We'll take care of Schulz.
     (To the others)
Come on.

They all follow Hoffy out, leaving Price and Sefton.

They stand for a while looking at each other. From
OFF come some WEIRD NOTES on the ocarina.

Joey sits in his bunk, playing on his new sweet potato.

                    SEFTON
That's the boy, Joey. Play us
a little something. What do you
want to hear, Price? Home On The
Range? Or maybe a little Wagner?

No answer from Price.

117

SEFTON
Or how about a game of pinochle?
No, you're not a pinochle man.
You're a chess player.
    (Moves to chess board)
I haven't played since I was a
kid. Let's see --
    (Maneuvers the white
     pieces)
-- a pawn moves this way, doesn't
it? And a bishop this way? And
the queen -- every which way,
doesn't it?

PRICE
Suppose you just sit down and keep
your mouth shut.

SEFTON
    (Moving about)
I went to school with a guy named
Price. But that was in Boston.
You're from Cleveland, aren't you.

PRICE
Yes, I'm from Cleveland.

SEFTON
I thought that's what you said.
You're from Cleveland. And you
were with the Thirty-sixth Bomb
Group?

PRICE
Thirty-fifth.

SEFTON
Three hundred and sixty-fifth
Bomb Squadron? Out of Chelveston?

PRICE
Are you questioning me?

SEFTON
Just getting acquainted.
Trying to make one friend in
this barracks.

PRICE
Don't bother, Sefton. I don't
like you. I never did and I
never will.

                         SEFTON
              A lot of people say that and the
              first thing you know is they get
              married and live happily ever
              after.
                    (Goes to window)
              I wonder what they're trying to
              pull out there?

74.   EXT. COMPOUND - (DAY)

      Several hundred P.O.W.s are casually strolling about
      the compound. The CAMERA MOVES TOWARDS the Administra-
      tion Building PAST an S.S. car parked on the roadway,
      with the motor running. An S.S. driver stands at the
      car door. Harry and Stosh stand by the car, inspect-
      ing it. CAMERA MOVES ON PAST the flagpole, against
      which leans Duke, and ON TO the porch of the Adminis-
      tration Building: there stands Hoffy, reading the
      bulletin board. Only he isn't reading it. From one
      corner of his eye he is peeking through the window
      into the Kommandant's office. Suddenly he reacts to
      a movement inside. Without turning, he gives the
      signal: he throws one end of his muffler around his
      neck.

      Duke, at the flagpole, gets it and throws his muffler
      around his neck, thusly relaying the signal.

      At the car, Harry follows suit.

      Marko, leaning against the north latrine, catches the
      signal and, still facing the compound, RAPS with his
      knuckles on the wooden boards.

75.   INT. NORTH LATRINE - (DAY)

      The Crutch is sitting on the wash trough. On hearing
      the RAPS, Bagradian pulls up The Crutch's loose pants'
      leg. Blondie strikes a match and lights the fuse on
      the smudge pot. Bagradian pulls down the pants' leg.
      They help The Crutch off the wash trough and he
      hobbles out.

76.   EXT. COMPOUND - (DAY)

      The Crutch is slowly hobbling toward the car, a thin
      wisp of smoke curling up from his pants' leg.

      Out of the Administration Building emerge two S.S.Men,
      leading Dunbar between them. Hoffy, standing at the

bulletin board, WHISTLES a few bars of the Air Force
song. Dunbar turns, sees Hoffy whistling. Hoffy
doesn't look at him, but Dunbar senses that something
is in the wind. He walks on between the S.S. Men.
As he is being led toward the car, still some thirty
feet away, P.O.W.s crowd in to watch him.

The Crutch, hobbling on from the direction of the
latrine, is some twenty feet from the car.

Duke straightens up from the flagpole casually, and
starts sauntering toward the car.

The latrine. Blondie and Bagradian have moved out of
the latrine and stand there with Marko, watching the
car.

Harry and Stosh at the car. Stosh tightening the belt
of his coat, Harry pulling the barracks cap tight on
his head.

The driver of the car opens the door. The S.S. Men
and Dunbar are some eight feet away now.

The Crutch, hobbling past the car, releases a string
and the smudge pot drops as he moves on. He barely
makes it. Almost instantly, there is a belch of fire
and smoke starts pouring out of the smoke bomb.

The wind billows the smoke across the car, rapidly
enveloping the S.S. Men and Dunbar. There are German
SHOUTS from within the smoke cloud.

Duke, Harry, Stosh, Blondie, Bagradian, Marko and
Hoffy move into the smoke from all sides. All now
is lost in smoke. Just silhouettes of men rushing
about. SHOUTS, German commands, SOUNDS of scuffling.
From OFF a siren starts to sound. German guards
come running from all corners of the compound into
the cloud.

In the goon towers, the guards wheel around their
machine guns, but don't dare to shoot into the smoke.

From the Administration Building storms von Scherbach,
followed by the two Lieutenants, Schulz and other
guards. They dash into the smoke cloud, which starts
lifting.

77.   THE COMPOUND - THROUGH THE WINDOW OF BARRACKS 4

The smoke cloud starts to clear. At the car, the
two S.S. Men and the driver stand with guns in their

hands. Dunbar is gone. The other P.O.W.s stand
around innocently. Von Scherbach is screaming his
head off, but his words are not heard. CAMERA PULLS
BACK INTO Barracks 4, revealing Sefton and Price at
the window. Sefton turns from the window, a little
smile on his face.

                    SEFTON
          Ach so!

                    PRICE
          What did you say?

                    SEFTON
          Amazing, what you can do with five
          thousand ping-pong balls, isn't it?

Price is pacing. Joey starts tootling again.

                    PRICE
               (To Joey)
          Stop that, will you!
               (To Sefton)
          Those idiots! So they sprang
          Dunbar! So what good is it?
          He's still in the compound, isn't
          he? How long can he last? Where
          can they hide him?

                    SEFTON
          Where. Up Joey's ocarina. Didn't
          you know?

Price looks at him.

DISSOLVE:

78. EXT. COMPOUND - (DAY)

All the P.O.W.s are formed into
a line that serpentines toward a
desk set up on the porch of the
Administration Building. Light
machine guns have been set up
around them, the guards watching
carefully. Behind the desk sit
the two German Lieutenants, and
in back of them stands Schulz.
Every P.O.W., as he passes, is
screened by the Lieutenants,
then dogtags and faces being
checked against an index of cards
and photographs on the desk.

                    COOKIE'S VOICE
          Yeah? Where did we
          hide him? Nobody knew
          that except Hoffy -
          not one of us - and he
          wouldn't talk. It
          sure drove the Krauts
          craxy looking for
          Dunbar. They herded
          us all out into the com-
          pound and put some extra
          machine guns on us and
          gave us the old picture
          check. You know,
          checking our dog-
          tags and our pans

Pirelli, Blondie, Hoffy and Duke file by. The next in line is Price, followed by Sefton. As Price is being checked, his eyes meet Schulz's. Schulz looks at him inquisitively. The only answer on Price's face for a split second is: "I don't know". But he's got to watch himself as he is followed by Sefton.

A barracks: Guards with dogs are searching under it.

Another barracks: German guards throw tear gas bombs into it and close the doors.

The compound. All the P.O.W.s are now lined up in long lines facing the Administration Building. Von Scherbach, standing on the porch flanked by the S.S. Men, his Lieutenants and Schulz, lets go with a tirade. THE CAMERA SWOOPS BACK from his face over the lined-up P.O.W.s all the way to the south latrine and UP AND OVER the water tank. As it now PANS INTO the water tank, we see Dunbar. He is hiding in the water tank, up to his knees in icy water. He is weak and drawn and he has to hold on not to collapse.

DISSOLVE:

COOKIE'S VOICE
against their index file. They searched under the barracks. They searched the roofs. They even searched the bathroom in the Kommandant's office, but no Dunbar. Then they tried to smoke him out, throwing tear gas bombs into every barracks, just in case he was hiding up in the rafters. Then they made us stand for six hours out there until finally von Scherbach came out and gave us his ultimatum: if Dunbar didn't come out by next morning he'd raze the whole lousy compound, stick by stick and if we'd sleep in the mud for the rest of our lives, that was okay by him. I thought he'd bust his gut the way he was screaming. He just couldn't figure how a guy could disappear from the compound and still be there, but Dunbar was there all right. He sure was there.

79.   EXT. COMPOUND - (NIGHT)

From the goon towers lights   COOKIE'S VOICE
are sweeping over the com-   He was there for
pound, the dark barracks   half the night, his
and the barbed wire fences.   feet right in the
                                    icy water. That's
80.   WATER TANK - ABOVE THE   tough to take,
        LATRINE - (NIGHT)   especially when you
                                    got three heated
Dunbar, exhausted, is cling-   pools at home.
ing desperately to the   It took a lot of
ladder inside the tank,   guts, the kind you'd
his feet in the icy water.   expect from a sergeant
Over the tank sweeps the   - but a lieutenant - !
light from a goon tower.

81.   EXT. BARRACKS 4 - (NIGHT)

The Hundefuehrer is leading his
dogs past the dark barracks. Not
a sound from within.

82.   INT. BARRACKS 4 - (NIGHT)

Blankets are hanging over the windows. On the center
table burns a ma:garine lamp. All the men from Barracks 4 are gathered around the table. All except
Joey and Sefton. In the center of the table is one
of the P.O.W.s' cap. The men, one by one, are dropping
their dogtags into it.

                        HOFFY
                  (Putting in his own
                    dogtag)
            Let's have it understood men -
            this is going to be a rough deal.
            But we have no choice. One of us
            must take Dunbar out of the camp
            tonight. Right away. We'll draw
            one dogtag and the guy who goes
            with it does the job. It's going
            to be rough because the Krauts have
            put on extra guards and they are
            expecting a move like this. So
            if anyone wants to withdraw, he
            better speak up now.

He looks around. Nobody moves.

                        HOFFY
            Then we're all in on it?

                        DUKE
            Everybody but Joey, and you know
            who.

They shoot a look towards Sefton. Sefton stands
leaning against his bunk. He looks right back at
them.

Back at the table.

                  HOFFY
    Okay.
         (With irony)
    Who's the lucky one?

He shakes the dogtags in the cap. Everyone crowds
around, tensely.

                  HARRY
    Let me do it, Hoffy.

                  STOSH
    You want to go?

                  HARRY
    No. I want to draw.

                  HOFFY
    All right.
         (Holding out cap)
    Draw.

Harry closes his eyes, puts his hand deep into the
cap and picks out a tag. But before anybody can
look at it, Price closes his fist over it.

                  PRICE
    Suppose we call this my tag.
    I'll take him out.

The men turn toward Price.

                  HOFFY
    No volunteers, Price. I said we're
    all in on it.

                  PRICE
    You have elected me Security.
    The way things have been going
    in this Barracks, I guess I've
    done a poor job and I want to
    make up for it. Is that asking
    too much?

Sefton, standing against the bunk, takes it in with
a grim smile.

                  HOFFY
    We've all done a poor job of it.

                         PRICE
          I still say this is my tag. Any
          objections, Hoffy?

                         HOFFY
          Any objections, men?

                         PIRELLI
          Not from me.

                         TRIZ
          He can have it.

                         HARRY
                    (To Stosh)
          Who are we to argue with a hero?

                         DUKE
          How about me latching on, Price?

                         HOFFY
          Three's a crowd, especially if
          you've got to cut your way through
          barbed wire.
                    (Hands Price wire
                     cutters)
          Here's the wire cutters.
                    (To Blondie)
          Are the civilian clothes ready?

                         BLONDIE
                    (Stuffing clothes into
                     duffel bag)
          Coming up.

                         HOFFY
                    (To Harry and Stosh)
          Get going on the trap door.

          They move to the old trap door and start unscrewing
          it. Price goes to his bunk, Hoffy with him. Price
          starts putting on his jacket.

                         PRICE
          What do you say, Hoffy. We'll
          hit the air raid trenches and
          cut out in back of Barracks nine.

                         HOFFY
          You'd better cut out in back of
          the south latrine.

                         PRICE
          Why the south latrine?

125

                    HOFFY
     Because that's where he is. In the
     water tank.

Price takes it smoothly.

                    PRICE
     Good spot. With any luck we'll
     make Krems by morning, or maybe
     even catch a barge to Linz.

Sefton, who has been watching closely, tosses two
packs of cigarettes on the table.

                    SEFTON
     Two packs of cigarettes say
     Dunbar never gets out of the
     compound.

                    HOFFY
     You starting that again?

                    SEFTON
     Anybody cover?

They all look at him.

                    STOSH
          (From the trap door)
     Somebody step on that crumb!

                    DUKE
     We warned you, Sefton!

                    SEFTON
     Sure you warned me. You were going
     to slit the throat of that stoolie.

He throws an open jack-knife onto the table. The blade
sticks. The knife quivers.

                    SEFTON
     Here's the knife to do it with.
     Only make sure you got the right
     throat.

                    DUKE
     We're looking at it.

                    HOFFY
          (To Harry and Stosh)
     Hurry up on that trap.
          (To Sefton)
     What are you trying to do, Sefton?
     Gum up the works?

                    SEFTON
That's right. Or would you rather
see Dunbar lying out there in the
mud tomorrow morning like Manfredi
and Johnson?

                    HOFFY
Look, Sefton, I had my hands full so
they wouldn't tear you apart --

                    SEFTON
I called it the last time, didn't I?

                    PRICE
Are we going to stand around here
and listen to him until the Germans
find out where Dunbar is?

                    SEFTON
The Germans know where Dunbar is.

                    HOFFY
How do they know?

                    SEFTON
You told them, Hoffy.

                    HOFFY
Who did?

                    SEFTON
You did!

                    HOFFY
You off your rocker?

                    SEFTON
Uh-huh. Fell right on my head.
     (Confronting Price)
Sprechen sie deutsch?

                    PRICE
No. I don't sprechen sie deutsch.

                    SEFTON
Maybe just one word? Kaput? Because you're kaput, Price.

                    PRICE
Will you get this guy out of my
hair so I can go?

                    SEFTON
Go where? To the Kommandant's
office and tell him where Dunbar
is?

                    PRICE
          (Starting for him)
I'll kill you for that!

                    SEFTON
Shut up!
          (Slaps his face)
Security Officer, eh? Screening
everybody, only who screened you?
Great American hero. From Cleveland,
Ohio! Enlisted right after Pearl
Harbor! When was Pearl Harbor, Price?
Or, don't you know?

                    PRICE
December seventh, forty-one.

                    SEFTON
What time?

                    PRICE
Six o'clock. I was having dinner.

                    SEFTON
Six o'clock in <u>Berlin</u>. They were
having lunch in <u>Cleveland</u>.
          (To the others)
Am I boring you, boys?

                    HOFFY
Go on.

                    SEFTON
He's a Nazi, Price is. For all I
know, his name is Preismaier or
Preissinger. Sure, he lived in
Cleveland, but when the war broke
out he came back to the Fatherland
like a good little Bundist. He
spoke our lingo so they put him
through spy school, gave him phony
dogtags --

                    PRICE
He's lying! He's just trying to get
himself off the hook!

                    HARRY
          (Jabbing him)
Shut up, he said.

                    STOSH
You heard him.

                    SEFTON
Okay, Herr Preismaier, let's have
the mail box.

                    PRICE
The what?

                    SEFTON
The one you took out of the corner of
your bunk and put in this pocket.

He snatches a black queen out of Price's coat pocket.

                    SEFTON
Now let me show you how they did it.
They did it by mail. That's right.
Little love notes between our Security
Officer and von Scherbach with Schulz
the mail man.
          (Ties up a loop
           in the light cord)
Here's the flag.
          (Opening a black queen)
And here's the mail box.
          (Grins at Price, who is
           sweating)
Cute, isn't it? They delivered the
mail or picked it up when we were
out of the barracks, like for Appell.
When there was a special delivery, they'd
pull a phony air raid to get us out of
here, like for instance, last night.
          (To Price again)
There wasn't a plane in the sky - or
was there, Price?

Price dives for the open trap door. He is caught by
Duke. He breaks away and flings himself at the
window, tearing down the blanket.

                    PRICE
          (Screaming)
Hilfe!

He never gets the whole word out. Stosh and Harry
jump him, Stosh clamping his hand over his mouth.
They throw him to the floor and all duck as the light
from the goon tower swoops through the barracks.

83.   EXT. COMPOUND - (NIGHT)

The Hundefuehrer, leading the dogs past Barracks Nine.
The dogs sense something, and bark. The Hundefuehrer
looks around. The dogs calm down and the Hundefuehrer
goes on.

84.   INT. BARRACKS 4 - (NIGHT)

Everybody is petrified. The barking dies down. Blondie
and Triz hang the blanket again.

                    HOFFY
               (Indicating Price)
          Gag him.

Two P.O.W.s move in and take over.

Duke moves up to Sefton.

                    DUKE
          Brother, were we all wet about you!

                    SEFTON
               (Putting a cigar butt into
                his mouth)
          Forget it.

He strikes a match on Duke's stubbled cheek and lights
the cigar. It doesn't hurt Duke a bit. He just
stands there with a broad grin.

                    HOFFY
               (Indicating Price)
          What are we going to do with him?

                    SEFTON
          Don't you know? Because I got my
          own ideas.
               (To Blondie)
          Let's have that civilian stuff.

Blondie gives him the barracks bag. Sefton opens it,
takes out a Tyrolean hat, puts it on. It is too small.

                    SEFTON
          I'll look pretty stupid in this,
          yodelling my way over those Alps.
          Now let's have the wire cutters.

Pirelli takes them out of Price's belt and gives them
to him.

                    HOFFY
You taking Dunbar?

                    SEFTON
You betcha. There ought to be some
reward money from Mama. Say ten
thousand bucks worth.

He starts putting on his jacket and his cap, the eyes
of every P.O.W. in the barracks on him.

                    SEFTON
I told you boys I'm no escape artist,
but for the first time, I like the
odds. Because now I got me a decoy.

                    HOFFY
What's the decoy?

                    SEFTON
Price. When I go I want you to
give me five minutes. Exactly
five minutes to get Dunbar out of
that water tank. Then you throw
Price out into the compound, nice and
loud. He'll draw every light from
every goon tower. It's our only
chance to cut through. What do you
say, Barracks' Chief?

                    HOFFY
Shoot!

Price squirms.

                    DUKE
What's the matter, Price? You said
you were going to save Dunbar, didn't
you? So now, you're getting your
chance.

Sefton has picked up the barracks bag and the wire
cutters and moves toward the trap door.

                    SEFTON
So long, Cookie. The department
store is all yours. What's left
of it.

                    COOKIE
So long, Sefton.

                    STOSH
You're not disposing of those
Russian broads?

> SEFTON
> Tell you what to do. First, get
> yourself a hundred cigarettes for
> the Kraut guards. Then get yourself
> another face.

Harry laughs.

> SEFTON
> You could use a new one yourself.

> HOFFY
> Let's synchronize the watches.
> Eleven forty-two, sharp.

> SEFTON
> (Adjusting his)
> Check.

He climbs down into the open trap. All the men crowd
around to say goodbye.

> SEFTON
> One more word. If I ever run into
> any of you bums on a street corner,
> just let's pretend we never met
> before. Understand?

He takes the cigar butt out of his mouth, puts it
into Duke's half-open mouth -- and goes. There is
a moment of silence.

> HOFFY
> This barracks will never be the same.

85.   UNDERNEATH BARRACK 4 - (NIGHT)

Sefton is crawling cautiously in the direction of the
latrine. Behind him, the trap door is being fitted
into the floor again.

86.   EXT. COMPOUND - (NIGHT)

Sefton has crawled to the edge of the barracks, waits
for a light to swoop by. Then he dashes into the
latrine just in time to evade another searchlight
from a goon tower.

87.   INT. LATRINE - (NIGHT)

Sefton recovers his breath, listens for a second, then
climbs up on the wash trough. He raps on the bottom
of the water tank.

88.   INT. WATER TANK - (NIGHT)

Dunbar, utterly exhausted, is clinging to the ladder,
his legs submerged in the icy water. He hears the
signal. There is a flicker in his eyes. He hears
another signal. With his last strength, he climbs
the ladder, waits for a light to swoop by, then works
himself over the top.

89.   INT. LATRINE - (NIGHT)

Sefton has climbed on a beam above the wash trough.
Dunbar's legs come down, dripping wet. Sefton gets
hold of them, then as Dunbar lets go above, he takes
his full weight and lowers him to the wash trough.
Dunbar lies there, gasping.

                    SEFTON
          Shut off the moaning, or we'll
          have the dogs on us. Shut it
          off, Lieutenant. This is orders!

                    DUNBAR
          My legs are frozen.

                    SEFTON
               (Rubbing his legs down)
          You'd better get that blue blood
          circulating, because we're busting
          out of this stink-hole in exactly --
               (Looks at watch)
          -- one minute and twenty seconds.

                    DUNBAR
               (Looking up)
          Sefton!

                    SEFTON
          What did you expect, a St. Bernard dog?

                    DUNBAR
          Not you.

                    SEFTON
          Want some brandy?

                    DUNBAR
          Yeah.

                              SEFTON
          Who doesn't! Suppose we wait until
          we hit the Waldorf Astoria.

                              DUNBAR
            It's on me.

                              SEFTON
          . You won't get off that cheap.

                              DUNBAR
          What are the chances busting out
          of here?

                              SEFTON
                    (Looking at his watch)
          We'll know in forty seconds.
                    (Then with a grin)
          Only in a democracy can a poor guy
          get his keister shot off with a rich
          guy.

90.   INT. BARRACKS 4 - (NIGHT)

        Hoffy stands looking at his watch. Blondie is cross-
        ing with the breadnife in his hand towards the door.
        Stosh and Duke hold the gagged Price down on the
        bunk. Harry has strung together some five old cans.

                              HARRY
                    (To the bearded P.O.W.)
          Hold his leg.

        The P.O.W. sits on Price's leg. Harry starts tying
        the tin cans to his ankle.

                              HARRY
                    (To Price)
          Just in case your Kameraden are
          hard of hearing.

                              HOFFY
          Fifteen seconds. Get him up.

        Stosh and Duke pull Price up off the bunk and move
        him to the door. He struggles and squirms.

                              STOSH
          Stop shaking, Price. There'll be
          no pardon from no governor.

                         DUKE
                    (To Price)
          Funny, ain't it? In your own
          Vaterland -- by your own Soldaten!
                    (To Stosh)
          The kid's got no sense of humor.

                         HOFFY
          What's the matter with you, Security?
          You were always so calm. Especially
          when you let Manfredi and Johnson
          go out there.
                    (To Blondie)
          Open the hatch.

Blondie has inserted the breadknife in the crack of
the door. He now whips up the knife with a sharp
movement.

91.   EXT. BARRACKS 4 - (NIGHT)

The bar across the door swivels up. The door is flung
open from inside. Duke and Stosh hold Price. Hoffy
tears the gag off his mouth.

                         HOFFY
               Let 'er go!

Duke and Stosh have lifted Price with all their might,
and give him a terrific heave. As Price comes flying
out into the compound, the tin cans clattering, the
door is slammed shut.

A light from a goon tower swings sharply to Price and
holds him in its beam. A burst of machine gun fire
splatters around him. He scrambles to his feet,
screaming.

                         PRICE
               Schiesst nicht! Schiesst nicht!
               Ich bin ein Deutscher!

His words are drowned out by more machine gun fire.
He tries to run back towards his barracks, but is cut
off by another beam and more machine gun fire from
another goon tower. He runs madly into the dark
compound, the tin cans clattering behind him - lights
from all the goon towers searching for him.

92.   <u>INT. LATRINE</u> - (NIGHT)

Sefton and Dunbar stand at the door of the latrine,
searchlights swinging in arcs toward the compound.
Sefton holds the wire-cutters in his hand. There is
the clatter of the tin cans and machine gun fire,
and Price's desperate screams, "Nicht schiessen!
Nicht schiessen!".

                    SEFTON
          Now!

They duck out.

93.   <u>EXT. COMPOUND</u> - (NIGHT)

Sefton and Dunbar dash across the short stretch to
the barbed wire. They fall on their faces at the
wire and Sefton starts cutting.

Price. A machine gun bullet has struck him in the
shoulder. He desperately tries to evade the relent-
less light beams. He manages to tear off the tin
cans, runs on towards the Administration Building.
A couple of more bullets hit him. He falls face
down into the mud. All the lights converge on him
and the machine guns sputter away.

94.   <u>BARBED WIRE</u> - (NIGHT)

Sefton is just cutting through the outer fence. In
back of him, Dunbar patches the cut wire of the inner
fence. Beyond them, all the lights play on the body
of Price. The machine guns are no longer shooting,
but there are whistles and a siren. The barking dogs
tear into Price's body.

Sefton and Dunbar crawl through the outer wire and
pause to patch it up hastily.

                    SEFTON
          Let's blow, Chauncey.

                    DUNBAR
          Let's!

They get to their feet and scramble off into the
forest.

95.   <u>EXT. COMPOUND</u> - (NIGHT)

Von Scherbach comes striding out of the Administration
Building followed by a Lieutenant, the two S.S. Men
and Schulz. He wades cockily through the mud with

his beautiful boots towards the body on the ground.
The Hundefueher calls off his dogs. The other guards
step back. With his boot, von Scherbach flips the
body over. The lights from the goon towers play on
the muddy face of Price. They all stand there stunned.

96.   INT. BARRACKS 4 - (NIGHT)

The lamps are being put out; the blankets being pulled
down by the P.O.W.s.

                    HOFFY
          All right, men. Everybody back
          in their bunks like nothing
          happened.

They climb into their bunks. All is still.

                    DUKE
          (Puffing Sefton's cigar)
          What do you know? The crud did it.

                    HARRY
          I'd like to know what made him do it.

                    STOSH
          Maybe he just wanted to steal our
          wire cutters. Ever think of that?

Cookie, in his bunk, a broad smile on his face, starts
whistling softly: When Johnny Comes Marching Home.
Beyond him lie all the P.O.W.s in the barracks, their
hearts beating, their eyes wide open.

97.   EXT. FOREST - (NIGHT)

Sefton and Dunbar climb swiftly up a hill through the
trees. Dunbar's arm is over Sefton's shoulder as they
march. OVER THIS, Cookie's whistling of Johnny Comes
Marching Home - gradually augmented by drums and then
an orchestra. Sefton and Dunbar march on, in time to
the music. SUPERIMPOSED BEYOND THEM appear the other
P.O.W.s from Stalag 17, their spirits marching with
them through the forest. Way in front, Stosh in his
underwear, waving a makeshift flag. Then comes Harry.
Then Cookie. Then Triz and Blondie. Then Joey, playing his ocarina in tune with the march, a smile on his
face. And Marko and The Crutch. Then Hoffy and Duke,
and all the others we have grown to know. All waving
their pathetic flags: towels, blankets and torn shirts.
All marching to freedom and home, marching with Sefton
and Dunbar. As the MUSIC SWELLS to a crescendo -

FADE OUT
                    THE END

Design:	Nicole Hayward
Compositor:	Star Type, Berkeley
Text:	10/15 Janson
Display:	Francis Gothic
Printer and binder:	Haddon Craftsmen, Inc.